MAX FACTOR

MAX FACTOR

The Man Who Changed
the Faces of the World

FRED E. BASTEN

Arcade Publishing
New York

FIRST EDITION

"Hooray for Hollywood," words by Johnny Mercer, music by Richard A. Whiting © 1937 (Renewed) WB Music Corp. All rights reserved. Used by permission of Alfred Publishing Co., Inc.

Library of Congress Cataloging-in-Publication Data

Basten, Fred E.
  Max Factor : the man who changed the faces of the world / Fred E. Basten. —1st ed.
      p. cm.
  ISBN 978-1-55970-875-3 (alk. paper)
    1. Factor, Max, 1872?–1938 2. Cosmetics industry—United States—Biography. 3. Cosmetics—United States. I. Title.
  TP983.A66F33 2008
  338.7'66855092—dc22
  [B]   2008006944

Published in the United States by Arcade Publishing, Inc., New York
Distributed by Hachette Book Group USA

Visit our Web site at www.arcadepub.com

10 9 8 7 6 5 4 3 2 1

Designed by API

EB

PRINTED IN THE UNITED STATES OF AMERICA

To Robert Salvatore

Contents

Author's Note

In writing this popular biography of Max Factor, the great cosmetics pioneer, I was fortunate to have complete access to the Factor archives: letters, scrapbooks, photos, and other biographical material, as well as company memos, sales bulletins, vintage newspaper and magazine articles, and so much more. All quotes in this book are taken from various sources in the archives.

Max Factor spoke in heavily accented English, and in interviews that date from prior to the mid-1920s, his words were transcribed phonetically ("is" became "iss," "maybe" became "mebbee," "people" became "pipple," and so on). In the interest of clarity, I have cleaned up Max's words so readers can focus on his meaning rather than on his accent and poor grammar.

One word Max always said clearly was "make-up," and from the moment he coined it, he spelled it with a hyphen. In deference to Max, that is how I have spelled the word throughout this book.

I worked for Max Factor and Company many years ago, as assistant to Len Smith, who was the head of the public relations department. It was a dream job: meeting and greeting visitors, sales representatives, dealers, and even dignitaries from around the world, showing them Hollywood, taking them to the studios to see movies being made, and introducing them to the stars. Max was no longer alive, but his spirit was everywhere. And the mere mention of his name triggered the most wonderful responses from everyone.

The year 2009 marks the hundredth anniversary of the company Max Factor founded. This book is a tribute to the man who came from near-poverty in Russia to become the very embodiment of the American dream.

MAX FACTOR

1

Escape

On a winter night in February 1904, twenty-seven-year-old Max Faktor huddled with his wife and three young children in a Russian forest, frightened more for the family he had kept secret for nearly five years than of the wind and snow or even the approaching czar's men calling his name. Only days earlier, Max Faktor was a favorite of the royal family and was esteemed by the royal court. Now he was being hunted as a fugitive.

Born in 1877 in Lodz, Poland, a town southwest of Warsaw with a developing textile industry, Max was one of ten children of Abraham and Cecilia Tandowsky Faktor. He never really knew his mother; she had died when he was a toddler. His father, a textile mill worker, worked long hours and was seldom home, so Max was raised by his older siblings. Little is known about his formal schooling, if indeed he had any. He did, however, have a Hebrew education — presumably at shul, studying the Talmud and Michnah — which he often neglected to help with the family finances. Although young Max dreamed of being an artist, at the age of seven he sold oranges, peanuts, and candy in the lobby of the

Czarina Theater in his hometown, a job he later called his "introduction to the world of make-believe."

A year later Max worked as an assistant to a local apothecary, a man who not only supplied remedies, potions, and pills to the sick and ailing but provided dental care as well. When Max told his siblings about the things he was seeing and touching, they made faces and turned away in disgust, but Max was fascinated and eager to learn more.

Soon after his ninth birthday he apprenticed to Lodz's leading wigmaker and cosmetician. For four years he trained in tying and weaving human hair into wigs, creating coiffures, and compounding and applying make-up, using local actors as models. "Catering to loveliness," as he put it, was Max's first full-time job.

It gave him the experience he needed to join the staff of the famed hairstylist and make-up creator, Anton of Berlin. Max's time with Anton soon led him to Moscow, where at age fourteen he was attached to Korpo, wigmaker and cosmetician to the Imperial Russian Grand Opera. For the next four years he traveled from city to city as make-up artist to some of the greatest operatic singers of the time. Whenever the company performed for Czar Nicholas II and the royal family, as well as other nobility, the temperamental opera stars insisted they look their absolute best. Max remembered being stormed backstage before royal performances, as each demanded to be made beautiful. Max worked calmly and quickly despite such pressure. Luckily, he was ambidextrous and equally skilled at using either hand. The performers usually met with royal approval. But not always.

The teenager was the company's scapegoat, no matter what went wrong. If the tenor missed his cue, Max's make-up was to blame. If the diva's performance was off, perhaps her eyebrows hadn't been arched to her liking. If the conductor misplaced his score, it was because Max had kept him waiting. As the months wore on, Max was saddled with even more responsibilities: hairdresser, prop boy, valet, gofer. His easygoing nature was often tested to the extreme, but Max took it all in stride. He was gaining valuable experience working with professionals and having his work admired by royalty.

Max remained with the Imperial Russian Grand Opera until his eighteenth birthday, when he was required by law to serve four years in the Russian army. Max wished to continue his theater work within the military, but the decision wasn't his. "The first day they picked me for the Hospital Corps," he recalled. "I was like a trained nurse. The doctor prescribed and I did the work. I did not like it but I learned much." He learned to bleed patients with cups and leeches and all he'd ever need to know about phrenology and skin disorders. During his years away his father remarried and his stepmother gave birth to a son they named John Jacob.

Max in his Russian army uniform, ca. 1890.

When Max's military service came to an end, he opened a small shop just outside Moscow, in the suburb of R'azan. Finding available space not far from the town square, Max, at twenty-two, became a proprietor, making and selling his own creams, rouges, fragrances, and wigs. For the first time in his life, he was working on his own and enjoying the responsibility and newfound freedom of being a shopkeeper. But all that changed when a traveling theatrical troupe passed through R'azan and a member of the company stopped at his little shop to buy some make-up. Unknown to Max, the troupe was on its way to Moscow to entertain the imperial family. Within weeks, Max's business took a royal upswing in sales and he was adopted by the summer court. It wasn't long before he was the cosmetician not only to Alexander Nicolaivich Romanoff, uncle to Czar Nicholas II, but also to the czar's personal physician and — once again — the Imperial Russian Grand Opera.

Max didn't want to return to the life he had known as a teenager working for the company, but he had no choice. His services had not been requested, they had been commanded. While Max was allowed to keep his shop, he knew he'd be forever on call, at the whim of the court favorites who wanted him to attend to their beautification, to create a new hairstyle, or to correct cosmetic problems, so that their eyes might sparkle, cheeks glow, and hair gleam when the czar of all Russia looked upon them. "All my attention went to their individual needs by showing them how to enhance their good points and conceal the less good," Max recalled years later.

Max was highly paid for his expertise, and he was constantly surrounded by the imperial family's dazzling wealth. He had never seen such an incredible display of jewelry — diamonds, rubies, emeralds, pearls — and gowns of velvet, silk, and satin. Soldiers and guards wore gold-braided uniforms, and armies of servants paraded about in exquisite liveries. Gigantic crystal chandeliers lit enormous rooms with polished parquet floors and Persian rugs. Curtains of sapphire and silver brocade hung from rods of gold at towering windows.

"I had but to ask and what I asked was mine," remembered Max, "but I was the same as a slave. The only thing I wanted was to be free." According to the strict rules of the czar's uncle, Max could not leave the court unescorted. "Every time I go out a dozen people watch what I am doing. They follow me. I have no life. I am only a creature to make beautiful the court, not to live myself."

Once a week Max was allowed to return to his store in R'azan for a few hours, attend to business there, and collect supplies, but he never made the journey alone. Guards accompanied him, then remained outside in the carriage, waiting stiffly for him. Max compared those visits to R'azan to being a prisoner on parole.

He bided his time with the court patiently, just as he had a few years earlier as a teenager waiting to join the army. But one day, during a weekly trip to his shop, a slight, dark-eyed young girl from Moscow came in with her chaperone. She looked into each of the cases, then up at Max — who was instantly captivated — and asked him questions about his various powders, creams, and perfumes. Once her chaperone was out of earshot, examining a new hairdressing and testing some rouge in the light of the front window, they talked — but not about cosmetics. Her name was Esther Rosa. She would return another time, she said, and she did, repeatedly, only on her return visits she would slip through the back of a friend's house next to the store. Max would enter through the front door, supposedly on business, while the guards outside waited in the carriage.

Max could think only of the hour or so a week he'd be able to spend with Esther, whom he called Lizzie. He hoped for more and despaired that their moments together were so scarce. He cursed the fate that made him a prisoner to beauty instead of his own man. Worse, he knew he was bound to the rule that forbade anyone in service to the court to marry or even be involved romantically without permission. Yet he told himself that love would find a way.

It was Lizzie who found a way. As Max entered their secret meeting place one day, she rushed to tell him that she had discovered a rabbi who had agreed to marry them without a license. No license meant no paperwork to fall into the wrong hands. The following week Lizzie and the rabbi, who had been smuggled into the house, were waiting for Max. The rabbi united the couple in a quiet, solemn ceremony, then silently exited, leaving Max and Lizzie alone together. It seemed like only an instant before Max had to break away from his tearful bride. "We must think only about this happy day," he told her, leaving her to return to the waiting guards. "Till death do us part," he had heard the rabbi say at the brief ceremony. A mockery, when a cruel court kept the newlyweds apart for all but one hour a week.

As the carriage made its way back to the palace, Max, sitting between his guards, fought to control his emotions. While he was thankful to the rabbi who had married them, he knew no rabbi could protect him from certain doom should the czar or his uncle learn of the marriage. He feared for his young bride. What would happen to her if the secret marriage were discovered? Was she safe? Max could only try not to arouse suspicion.

There were times in the months ahead when Max was unable to see Lizzie, when the calendar was so crowded with events he simply could not get away. Once their children were born — first Freda, then Cecilia, then Davis — he agonized at not being able to live with his young family. There was no way Lizzie could bring the little ones to their secret meeting place and no way the carriage would stray from its familiar route to his shop in R'azan. He dreaded the thought of having his children grow up without a father. He knew how his own father had struggled.

There were other, more serious dangers. At the beginning of Nicholas II's reign, the Jewish population in the Russian Empire exceeded five million. By the early 1900s, the number had grown considerably despite the exodus of over a million Jews to

The Factor family (left to right: Lizzie, Freda, Cecilia, Max, and Davis), taken shortly before fleeing to America, 1904.

other countries, mainly America, to escape poverty and persecution. Famine was common, and religious persecution was on the rise with the enactment of strict anti-Semitic legislation.

The Jews in Russia were never thought of as Russians. They were regarded as interlopers. But the Jewish people were not responsible for their increase in numbers on Russian soil. By annexing surrounding territories with significant Jewish populations, such as the Ukraine and Poland, Russia herself was to blame. In towns big and small within southwestern and western Russia, many essential members of the communities — tailors, apothecaries, shoemakers, glaziers, pub-keepers, cabinetmakers — were Jewish. Peasants depended largely on Jewish middlemen for the sale of their goods and produce, as well as their connections with suppliers of necessities. Jewish peddlers were familiar and indispensable figures.

Nicholas II feared a rise in Jewish power. If the Jews became stronger, he believed, they would overthrow the government. Although the royal family lived in seclusion, constantly protected by secret police and military guards, he felt his life, or his way of life, was threatened. In 1903 he ordered a siege on the Jews he so feared and hated, and burned down their villages. It was only the beginning.

Max knew his services were invaluable to the court, but he also knew his time was coming. His brother Nathan and uncle Fischel had already left Russia for a city called St. Louis in America, a land that promised freedom, happiness, and opportunity. St. Louis would play host to the World's Fair in the coming year, and Max wanted to be part of it. Perhaps he could exhibit his wares at the fair. Max dreamed of going to America, where he and his family could live openly together. But how could he make that happen? It seemed impossible.

Overworked and under pressure from the constant surveillance, Max began to lose weight. He had always been of small stature — barely five feet tall — and slight build. Most of the court didn't notice; they saw only themselves. Max had made a good friend at court, a general, whom he felt he could trust. Rarely in Moscow, the general had returned from the field to see the beautician looking poorly and troubled. He invited Max to speak with him privately, away from the guards.

Max finally shared his dangerous secret: about the girl he loved, the clandestine marriage, his young children, and his dream of America. The general listened quietly, then told Max it would be arranged.

The following day at court, the general remarked that the cosmetician looked ill and what a catastrophe it would be for the courtiers, what with the coming season of grand pageants and balls hosted by the czar at the palace.

The next morning Max had a visit from the general's personal physician. Max's face, arms, and hands were sallow; covered with a yellowish make-up, he looked jaundiced. The doctor reported to the court on the patient's poor appearance. With a mind to its hair, face, and complexion, the court unanimously recommended a stay of ninety days in Carlsbad, the centuries-old Bohemian spa famed for its thermal springs and healing waters, where ailing court members were often sent to recuperate. The doctor gave Max the news and left. The general told Max to be ready to leave for Carlsbad in the morning. He would arrange for Lizzie and the children to meet Max there. The rest would be up to Max.

Max was accompanied to Carlsbad by his guards. As the train pulled into the valley, he saw that the surrounding forested hills were covered with snow. Despite the cold, steam rose from the waters of the Tepla River, which ran through town. Magnificent castles and manors dotted the countryside. In the near distance was a beautiful church. It was still morning, but scores of people were milling about, many drinking from porcelain mugs. Max wondered how and where he would find his family. How long would his guards stay with him? But no sooner had he departed the train than the guards crossed the tracks for the return trip to Moscow. He limped weakly ahead with his bags, just in case they were still watching. He kept looking back until they were gone.

Max walked to the town center. In the main square by a fountain he spotted four figures huddled together against the cold. She was bundled from head to foot, but he instantly recognized the tallest figure. His limp disappeared as he ran to Lizzie and the children. They had a long moment in each other's arms, then they were off to the forest that flanked Carlsbad. Max knew it would only be hours, at most, before the palace was notified that he hadn't checked into the spa.

Lizzie had not slept since she received word from the general. She had gone to Max's shop in R'azan, taken as many of his products as she could carry, then packed food and blankets. Now she and Max and the youngsters were trudging through snow in the forest. They walked mainly at night when they were less likely to be detected, traveling seemingly endless miles until they reached a clearing in the woods. Ahead was a seaport where the steamship *Molka III* was boarding for America. Max happily paid the fare. Money was not a problem. Over the years, he had saved nearly $40,000, which he carried with him in a pouch. At last they were aboard and on their way.

Years later, whenever Max retold the story of his escape from Russia, he always closed by saying, "Thank God, there were no passports to America then."

2

A New World

As the *Molka III* departed the harbor on February 13, 1904, Max and his family were enjoying the seclusion and warmth of their small cabin below deck. They remained there throughout the night and early morning, still uncertain about their safety. Max was worried that someone might have followed them onboard, but no one had knocked on their door, and the ship was at sea, well away from the ordeal they had left behind.

When Max finally led Lizzie and the children outside their cabin, they joined a mass of people, young and old; some still huddled together, others off by themselves as much as was possible; some nicely dressed in the winter fashions of the day, others bundled in tattered garb, and still others in clothing from places unfamiliar to Max. The passengers were speaking different languages, and some milled about with expressionless faces, as though uncertain about what they had left behind and what was to come in the new country. But there were no guards, no eyes watching them suspiciously. For the first time in years, Max could relax.

He met a fellow traveler who not only spoke his native Polish but German, Russian, and English as well. The young man seemed bright and ambitious, and was eager to see the country that would become his new home. Max told him about the St. Louis World's Fair and how he wanted to be a part of it. He also admitted his concern about being unable to speak or understand English, which might hamper his chances of participating. Would the young man be interested in helping him establish a place at the World's Fair? he offered. By the time the *Molka III* neared America's eastern coastline, Max had a partner for his hoped-for venture in St. Louis. The fellow even offered to help finance Max's exhibit at the fair.

As the ship entered New York harbor, passengers scrambled to the top deck to see the towering Statue of Liberty as it welcomed the newcomers with its promise of freedom. Although a large number of people had appeared downtrodden throughout the voyage, they suddenly took on a new spirit and dignity. Many who had endured the trip in steerage rushed topward in their finest folk costumes.

The Faktors arrived in America at the beginning of a peak period that saw an average of five thousand immigrants streaming into the country daily. For the privileged, the inspection process was simple. First- and second-class passengers, which included Max, his family, and new partner, were hurriedly inspected on-board, then instructed to pass through customs on the pier. After that they would be free to enter the United States. Max did not know what was happening to another group, the third-class and steerage passengers, who were being transported from the pier by ferry to Ellis Island out in the harbor.

Max's new partner explained that those with less would be examined more closely, medically and legally, because the government believed they were more likely to be carriers of disease or lawbreakers. Inversely, those with greater resources were less likely to end up in institutions, hospitals, or jails, and become burdens to the state. Some on the ferry were granted entry; others were sent back to their respective countries. To have come so far, to have spent so long deep down in the ship, crowded together, frightened, and probably in filth, only to be turned away . . .

Max and his family walked down the ramp to the customs inspector's desk. Max didn't know how to tell the inspector that he had misspelled their name, so from then on, he was Max FACTOR.

His first impression of New York was not favorable. "A terrible place of crowds and noise . . . a frightening place where hordes charged up and down at a furious pace, jabbering in an unknown tongue." He stopped a young man on the street. "I asked him if there was any place in America without so many people in it, and not going someplace so quick." Max had spoken in Polish. The man simply shrugged and kept going.

Max's group, now numbering five, boarded a horse-drawn trolley that took them to an imposing building on 43rd Street and Lexington Avenue. High above on one of the building's corners perched a monumental eagle with outspread wings, as if to take flight. They had arrived at Grand Central Station.

Inside, the air smoky from the steam engines, Max could only marvel at the congestion in the big hall. He couldn't get on the train to St. Louis fast enough. The journey took two days. Once there, he settled his family in a small rear apartment on Washington Street, near his brother Nathan and uncle Fischel, then set out with his partner to get exhibit space at the fair. At such a late date, only weeks before the fair's much-publicized opening, the demand among exhibitors was overwhelming. Originally scheduled to open on April 10, 1903, the one hundredth anniversary of the Louisiana Purchase, it had to be delayed by a year as the scope of the exhibition broadened and, with it, interest among exhibitors. Nothing was available in or near the prime locations, but there was an opening at the Palace of Varied Industries and Manufacture. The area was tiny and away from the main walkways, but Max was grateful to have it. There was much work to do to ready his exhibit. He was anxious to introduce his products to America, particularly his switches and curls, hairpieces that were in great demand among the fashionable women of the day.

The St. Louis World's Fair, officially known as the Louisiana Purchase Exhibition, claimed to be the largest, most beautiful, and most exciting international exhibition the world had ever known. The fairgrounds were spread across twelve hundred acres to showcase over fifteen hundred spectacular buildings, including Beaux-Arts palaces and fountains, all of which were lavishly illuminated at night by electric lighting — a recent innovation at the turn of the century. It seemed as if all of America's states and every nation on earth were represented, including Russia. Learning that he was one of over six hundred Russians at the fair, Max began to worry. But once he discovered that the others were artists and entertainers, singers and dancers, people he had known from his days in the Russian theater, he relaxed. He felt even better when he heard that the Russian imperial government had abstained from taking official part in the fair, leaving its subjects free to exhibit in the way that suited them best. According to the fair's handbill, the performing Russians presented their program "with brave sprightliness in spite of their sorrow at home."

A mile-long arcade called the Pike held fifty different carnival amusements from faraway places, such as the Dancing Girls of Madrid, Turkey's Whirling Dervishes, and belly dancers from the mysterious Middle East. The expression "coming down the pike" originated at the fair, as visitors never knew what they'd see next: an elephant water slide; a towering bear sculpture made entirely of prunes; a statue in butter of President Theodore Roosevelt, who attended the fair; or a darkened room that offered the inquisitive a first look, lasting only a few minutes, of a new entertainment — pictures that moved, shown on a makeshift screen.

Ice-cream cones were invented on the spot when one of the booths ran out of paper plates. The enterprising proprietor borrowed wafer-thin waffles from the next booth, rolled them up, and filled them with ice cream. The famous product of the Far East Tea House was going untouched because of the sweltering heat, so hot tea was poured over ice cubes, creating the most popular drink at the exposition. And a new song was sweeping the nation, "Meet Me in St. Louis."

The fair wasn't the only attraction in St. Louis that summer. Another event, one of less importance by comparison, was held from August 29 through September 3: the Olympic Games! It was only the third Olympics of modern times, this one following Athens in 1896 and Paris in 1900. It was not yet a competition between nations but one between amateur athletes from around the world, who had to pay their own way to St. Louis, as well as all their own expenses. Of the 681 athletes in attendance, 525 were from the United States, and most of the rest were from Canada. The intense heat caused several of the events to be canceled; another was rerun because of a dispute between the two top finishers; and still another was highlighted by an American gymnast with only one leg who finished the games with two gold, two silver, and one bronze medal. The most controversial event of the games was the marathon. First to cross the finish line was a New Yorker named Fred Lorz, who was crowned with a laurel wreath by Alice Roosevelt, the president's daughter, as the crowd cheered. He was about to receive his medal when it was learned that Lorz had traveled half of the marathon in a car, rejoining the race near the end!

By the time the fair closed on December 1, 1904, an average of more than a hundred thousand new visitors came to the fairgrounds each day, only to return again and again, and an estimated total of twenty million during its seven-month run. Max Factor was exhausted. He had worked a six-day week each and every week, missing only Sundays when the fair was closed. Max and his partner had labored late into the evenings with few breaks, catering to the steady flow of people who stopped by their booth to see the cosmetics, perfumes, combs, and hair products created by the former beautician to Russia's royal family. Only one event took Max away from the fair. On August 18 he was home when Lizzie gave birth to their fourth child, a son they named Frank.

Max had invested most of his money into the venture at the fair, paying for the space, equipment, and supplies. Business had been excellent, better than expected; a good profit had been made. But when Max went to close his exhibit once the fair had ended, his partner didn't show up to help him. The shelves were bare and the money pot was empty. Max was heartbroken. He had trusted the young man who had worked shoulder to shoulder with him for months, answering questions from visitors and handling sales while Max was busy creating hairstyles and compounding his powders and other cosmetics. His partner had spoken with most of the customers. Only occasionally did Max chat with a visitor in Polish or Russian, even German, which he had picked up while working for Anton in Berlin. Max's English was improving, but he was unsure of himself and his accent was heavy. He never really learned to read or write English properly. In the years ahead he relied on his children to translate for him.

Max knew he wouldn't have been able to operate his exhibit without his partner, and he was grateful for having met him, but now he was left with little to show for his venture. What next?

Max was not lacking in confidence. He knew he was a master cosmetician, and could style and cut hair to perfection. Cosmetics were his driving interest, but aside from stage performers, few people, if any, wore make-up. There was money to be made in cutting hair, however. He ruled out women, since most wore their hair long in the Victorian style of the day. He knew men would return week after week for a cut or a trim and a shave.

With help from his brother and uncle, Max opened Factor's Barber Shop at 1513 Biddle Street, and moved his family into a small apartment over the shop. Max attracted the attention of his neighbors from the start. Few customers had the luxury of plumbing, but they could bathe in Max's basement for twenty-five cents before going upstairs for a shave and a haircut, maybe even a shampoo, a nose and ear trim, a manicure, or a facial with a splash of Bay Rum.

*Max (at right) with two assistants and four-year-old Davis
in the doorway of his St. Louis barbershop, 1906.*

As Max's business flourished, tragedy suddenly struck. On
March 17, 1906, Lizzie fell dead on the sidewalk two blocks away
from her home. The next day the *St. Louis Globe-Democrat* reported that her death was "presumably from heart disease," but

a brain hemorrhage was later determined as the cause. Max rarely saw his children, in Russia and while he was away at the fair; now their mother was gone.

Max was at a loss. Then he remembered a family he had known in Russia, the Sradkowskas, who had several daughters. Although the sisters were much younger than Max, they were of age, particularly Huma, whom he favored. Huma was the creative one who spent hours sewing delicate fashions for her beloved doll collection. As a teenager she tutored the children of wealthy families. Max wrote Huma's parents to ask for her hand in marriage. A letter of consent arrived within a month. Huma was on her way to St. Louis.

Huma Sradkowska and Max Factor were married on August 15, 1906. Their first year together seemed ideal, but following the birth of their son, Louis, the relationship began to fall apart. Huma, or Helen, as Max called her, may have doted on her doll collection, but motherhood proved too challenging. Caring to baby Louis's needs made her irritable, and she soon ignored the other children in the family. She resented Max for separating her from her own family and the boy she loved back home; she embarrassed him in front of customers in his shop, striking him and calling him obscene names. She stole jewelry from the kids, took rings off the baby's fingers, and pawned them. She disappeared for long periods, spent nights on the town (with other men, Max suspected), and never explained her whereabouts. Weeks went by without her saying a word or lifting a finger around the house; she sat sulking, doing nothing. Finally, he'd had enough; Max filed for divorce. Helen bitterly fought back with slanderous accusations — court records on file in St. Louis show that she claimed Max was not the father of Louis — which were proven to be false. Following a nasty yearlong court battle, Max was awarded custody of his five children.

Max had difficulty keeping his barbershop open during and after his ordeal with Helen. He had to care for the children as well. Freda, Cecilia, and Davis were a big help, but they were now old enough to attend school, so Max often brought young Frank and baby Louis to work. He also hired two assistants; having two trained barbers in the shop freed him to check on his children. The last thing he needed during this trying time was someone at the door looking for a handout.

John Jacob Factor was Max's teenage half brother, born while Max was in the Russian army. Although Max had learned of his father's remarriage and the new addition to the family, Jacob was a virtual stranger. Nevertheless, hearing that Jacob had come to St. Louis to learn a trade, Max took him in and taught him the art of barbering. The youngster caught on quickly and added a few moves of his own, fast-talking his customers, distracting them so he could add "extras" and build up his tab. Young, brash, and fiercely independent, Jacob soon announced that he had learned enough to open a small barbershop of his own — just down the street! There would be two Factor barbershops within walking distance! Max was furious and vowed to have nothing more to do with Jacob.

It wasn't until a sympathetic neighbor offered to tend to Max's children that his luck began to change. She had Old World charm and the youngsters adored her. So did Max. On January 21, 1908, Max and Jennie Cook were married. His home life happy again, Max grew restless with his work. His barbershop was profitable, but barbering had never been his dream, and he hadn't come to America just to cut hair. His customers first put the seed of an idea into his head when he heard them talking about a newfangled form of entertainment called "photoplays." He had heard people talk about it at the fair, too, but thought it was nothing more than a novelty.

More and more people were talking, this time about real photoplays they had seen, moving pictures that told a story, if only briefly. One had everyone excited. It was only nine minutes long, but the action on the screen had them gasping. *The Great Train Robbery* was released in 1904 but had only recently come to St. Louis along with several other photoplays.

Max suddenly paid attention to the barbershop talk. Were they like slide shows? he wanted to know, referring to a popular home entertainment of the day. Not at all, he was told. These weren't stills. These pictures ran together; people and things moved, just as in real life.

Max had to see for himself. One afternoon he took a break from the barbershop to travel downtown, where he sat in a darkened room on folding chairs with twenty or so other people. The "movies," as they came to be known, were crude, but he enjoyed what he saw. So much entertainment for only a nickel!

All the photoplays had been made in New York, New Jersey, or Chicago, but filmmakers were heading west, where the weather was better and the outdoor scenery offered a greater variety of landscapes. Intrigued, Max began to wonder if his future might be in selling wigs, hairpieces, and cosmetics to the performers in these pictures. If he was to make a move, now was the time. He had taken many risks in his life. Why not one more?

3

Starting Over

In 1908 Los Angeles was on its way to becoming the most populated city on the West Coast, edging closer to San Francisco with each passing day. The reason for its surging growth was the railroads, which had finally reached Southern California from the east. The hub of activity was downtown, where many businesses were staking their claim in the city. Within the next few years a new industry — the film industry — would create its own surge.

Downtown Los Angeles was a bustling, crowded place with buildings ten stories high, even higher. Mansions stood atop Bunker Hill, which overlooked the business district. Angel's Flight, "the shortest railroad in the world," took residents on a one-minute ride up and down the steep incline from Third and Hill streets for only one penny. Everyone else took a streetcar downtown, where they worked, shopped, or went to the theater. Theatergoing was a major entertainment; the public flocked to see actors in live dramas, singers and dancers in musicals, and talented performers who came to town with their vaudeville acts.

Soon after his arrival on October 11, 1908, Max opened a tiny shop at 1204 South Central Avenue on the edge of downtown. The sign above the entrance read "Max Factor's Antiseptic Hair Store.

21

Toupees made-to-order. High-grade work." While it mentioned only his hair products, he also stocked several lines of theatrical make-up. He was the West Coast distributor for both Leichner and Minor, manufacturers of the top brands of greasepaint for theater performers, but he carried his own line of make-up for the theater as well: face powder, rouge, cleansing cream, and lip rouge, which his children helped package. The stage people were pleased to discover Max's store so close to where they were performing. Less than three months after the opening, on January 2, 1909, he founded Max Factor and Company. Within the first year Max had not only established a foothold in L.A.'s downtown area but name recognition for his own label among the entertainers.

By early 1910 the city's budding film industry received it's biggest boost when the Biograph Company sent director D. W. Griffith to Los Angeles. Along with Griffith came his troupe of actors, including Lillian Gish, Mary Pickford, Jack Pickford, Henry B. Walthall, Blanche Sweet, Lionel Barrymore, and the "Biograph Girl," Florence Lawrence. Dozens of filmmakers followed, along with their players, and soon it wasn't unusual to see one-reelers (which ran about twelve minutes) being shot in vacant lots, along alleys running behind storefronts, on the rooftops of office buildings, even on city streets. The public didn't know the actors' names then, but they would before long.

One day Max saw a group of people passing his store window looking "ghoulish," as he remembered. He followed them down the street to an empty lot where a platform had been set up. Half of the group climbed onto the platform, gesturing and making faces, then pushing each other and fighting as if in a bar brawl. Max asked one of the men standing by what was going on.

A movie, he was told. The man explained that the actors first rehearsed the scene, then shot it. Max wanted to know what they had on their faces. Some were using stage make-up, while others wore concoctions they had made themselves: odd mixtures of Vaseline and flour, lard and cornstarch, or cold cream and paprika. The more adventurous had even tried ground brick dust mixed

with Vaseline or lard to get a flesh-colored look. Max invited them
to drop by his store. A few did but saw nothing they hadn't tried
before, even Leichner's top-of-the-line imported greasepaint in
stick form.

As more movie people visited Max's store, he learned that
they needed something different from stage make-up, which was
much too heavy. Stage make-up had to be applied one-eighth of
an inch thick, then powdered. When it dried it formed a stiff
mask and often cracked, which wasn't a problem in the theater
where audiences were seated far away from the performers, but
onscreen, especially in close-ups, it didn't work. Even hairline
cracks were visible. What the actors needed was a make-up that
allowed them to show expression without cracking and something
with enough tints to give them a natural look, not a mask.

At the back of his store on South Central Avenue, Max had
set up a little chemical laboratory, just as he had in Europe and in
every store he had ever operated. He spent countless hours there,
starting at the end of each workday in the store and continuing
late into the evenings, formulating and testing theatrical make-up
in an effort to adapt it for motion picture use. He often abandoned
his store for the lab, leaving his wife and children to attend to
business. But the arrival of director Cecil B. DeMille in the sleepy
village of Hollywood in 1913 put a hold on Max's experimenta-
tions and turned him in another direction.

According to legend, DeMille had come from Arizona, where
he'd been shooting the large-scale western *The Squaw Man*. Un-
happy with the location, he continued westward, winding up in
Hollywood. But documents discovered by Betty Lasky, the
daughter of the film's producer, Jesse L. Lasky, revealed that
Lasky had sent DeMille directly to Hollywood from New York to
scout a location for the new West Coast offices of the Jesse L.
Lasky Feature Play Company. Lasky was interested in acquiring
a weather-beaten barn in an orange grove at Selma Avenue and
Vine Street, where he would set up his studio and film his first
feature production, to be codirected by his best friend, Cecil B.

DeMille, and Oscar Apfel. Partnered with Lasky in this venture was his brother-in-law, Samuel Goldfish (later known as Sam Goldwyn), a onetime glove salesman.

By then Max Factor had seen enough movies to know that the materials filmmakers were using for wigs, beards, and mustaches were unacceptable, so bad that they were laughable. Max felt that expertly crafted real hair — grade-A human hair — should be used, not clumsy substitutes such as straw, mattress stuffing, excelsior, Spanish moss, wool, tobacco leaves, even mohair stuffing from Model-T Fords! One actor admitted to Max that his face had been painted with mucilage then dabbed with sand and tobacco flakes for a stubble-beard effect.

Max realized that the movie men, many of whom were just getting started in a new profession, had barely enough money to spend on performers, let alone hair products, especially when barely seen in long shots. He knew the odds were against him, but he was determined to speak with DeMille.

Production on *The Squaw Man* had begun; scenes were being filmed on an outdoor stage behind the old barn. Max learned that other scenes were still to be shot on nearby locations, including Los Angeles, Hemet, Palomar, and Sun Valley in the San Fernando Valley. DeMille introduced Max to Oscar Apfel, cameraman Alfred Gandolfi, and the leading players, Dustin Farnum and Winifred Kingston.

At five feet eleven, DeMille towered over the diminutive Max Factor. DeMille had the presence of a commander, but Max was not intimidated. He had faced far more powerful men in Russia, and had earned their respect and admiration for his flawless creations. He didn't back down even when DeMille initially rejected his proposal. Max showed him examples of his handmade wigs, mustaches, beards, and goatees, all crafted with human hair. DeMille commented on the remarkable workmanship, the look and feel of each sample, but ultimately held firm. He wished he could use them, he said, but he couldn't spare the expense. He suggested renting them.

Cecil B. DeMille

Max had never considered this before. Renting his valuable hairpieces presented problems. Would DeMille be willing to give him a hefty deposit? Could the director guarantee the wigs would be returned in reusable condition at the end of a day's filming? Who would be responsible for the costly wigs on set?

Max had an idea. He would rent the wigs without a deposit if DeMille used his sons — Davis, Louis, and Frank — as extras. The boys could keep an eye on the wigs, ensure that none were lost or damaged, and collect them at the end of each day. As extras, they would also be paid the usual three dollars a day, unless they returned without all the wigs. The cost of missing wigs would be deducted from their pay.

DeMille agreed. Max had his first movie-director customer, and the Factor boys became "Hollywood Indians." The youngsters were thrilled, until they realized they had to be up before dawn to be trucked miles into the Hollywood Hills. As Frank Factor remembered, "We would smear some of my father's darkest make-up over our bodies and faces, throw a gaudy blanket over our shoulders, slip on one of the several dozen wigs we had brought with us, practice our war whoops, then grab some bows and arrows and go swooping down on innocent white settlers with murder in our looks and actions." Frank and Louis were never frontline performers in these "massacres" because they weren't big enough to pass for full-grown Indian braves. Davis however, was, so he occasionally saw front-row action.

It was exciting and fun for the boys, except for one thing: they had never been on horses before. Worse, unlike cowboys who rode saddled horses, the Indians rode bareback. Staying on the horses was tough enough, but the pain from riding bareback was almost unbearable. The boys had to find a way out, and it was Davis who devised a way. "When you hear the first muskets go off," he told his younger brothers, "throw your hands up in the air, scream a few times, grab your chest where the bullets are supposed to go through, then fall off the horse. Bang, three Jewish Indians are dead!" It worked for a while, until they started hurting themselves.

The real solution was to not get on a horse at all. Max didn't mind, neither did DeMille, so long as the boys gathered the wigs at the end of the day. Staying on horseback might have been easier at times. As Davis told it, "The Hollywood Indians could never be persuaded to bring in their wigs folded neatly before turning them back to us. Nearly all of them came riding in, whooping and hollering, whipping off their hairpieces, and tossing them in the air as they rode. So the three of us had to go out and pick them up. Sometimes we had to walk a mile or more before we found all of them. It wasn't too difficult to locate the wigs in open spaces, but sometimes there were trees around. Those demonical extras would almost always fling their wigs up in the branches, and we'd have to shinny up after them."

One late afternoon Frank was high in a walnut tree when a branch gave way. He fell to the ground and broke his arm. Knowing they had to return with the wig, Davis begged off, claiming he was too heavy to go after it, so little Louis got the job. That should have been the end of the Factor boys' career as "actors," but it wasn't. Frank claimed that between 1913 and 1916 they appeared in more Wild West movies than any other real actors in town. It was because their father's hairpieces were being requested by more and more filmmakers.

The Squaw Man, released February 15, 1914, was the first feature film made in Hollywood. Produced at a cost of $21,600, it earned a profit of $244,700. A huge hit in its day, the movie not only jump-started the career of Cecil B. DeMille, it showed producers and audiences alike that realistic wigs were instrumental to the success of films.

Long before the release of *The Squaw Man*, Max Factor returned to his lab, where he continued to work on make-up specifically for the movies. He became increasingly dependent on his children for help. During summers and after school, Max's sons and two daughters comprised the staff of the small store. It wasn't long before the boys were attending barber school and the girls were learning about hairdressing and make-up and how to apply it. Max taught them the art of wigmaking; and the children milled face powder in hand-cranked machines, as well as ground and mixed ingredients for all the other cosmetic products. They filled jars and bottles and licked labels.

Two of the boys, Davis and Frank, even became entrepreneurs. For several years, on Halloween, New Year's Eve, and other festive occasions, they earned extra money by making false beards and mustaches and selling them to merrymakers on the downtown streets. "Some of our school friends helped us to sell them," Davis confessed, "until my father put a stop to it. He discovered that a few of the older boys were charging only fifteen cents, a fortune to them but not to Father." But Max was forgiving. As business steadily expanded, Max recruited assistants for the manufacturing plant from among the boy's schoolmates. Several of those boyhood friends who worked for the company in the early days later became members of the firm.

The long months Max had spent in his lab formulating, testing, and experimenting with theatrical make-up for motion picture use finally came to an end in 1914. He had created a greasepaint in cream rather than stick form, ultra-thin in consistency, completely flexible on the skin, and produced in twelve precisely graduated shades. Max had tested it repeatedly on actor Henry B. Walthall before its introduction.

Surprisingly, it was not the dramatic actors who first took advantage of Max Factor's new "flexible greasepaint" but the comedians of the day — Charlie Chaplin, Buster Keaton, Ben Turpin, Roscoe "Fatty" Arbuckle, Louise Fazenda, Charlie Murray, Ford Sterling, among others. They came to the Factor store initially skeptical of the new product but willing to try it nonetheless. They returned not only to give Max their enthusiastic approval but to have him personally apply the new make-up. Because the cream product differed so radically from the old greasepaint, they had to be shown the proper application.

It wasn't long before other screen actors were making their way to Max's little store, such rising popular stars as Marie Dressler, Mabel Normand, Clara Kimball Young, William Farnum, John Barrymore, Polly Moran, Richard Bennett, Geraldine Farrar, and the Talmadge sisters, Constance and Norma. One of the few holdouts was Tom Mix, a real-life cowboy and gun-toting Texas Ranger, who felt wearing make-up was "too sissy." But once he gave in to what he called "the make-up ordeal" and saw how much stronger his features became in the hands of Max Factor, he went from star to superstar and one of the highest-paid actors of the silent screen.

With demand increasing and because his customers had to be made up and ready early for the day's filming, Max began

*Real-life cowboy
Tom Mix and his
horse, Tony.*

opening his store at 5:30 a.m. There was also a growing number of performers who now wanted to be made up on location or at their studios.

Until 1914, Max and his son Frank traveled together by streetcar for work. Max never learned how to drive, so he also depended on trolleys, buses, and his bicycle. Once asked why he took public transportation everywhere, he replied, "Because I don't have a rich father like my sons." As the years went on, however, he depended on his son Louis, who acted as his chauffeur.

Getting to various locations wasn't always easy for Max. One especially hectic day had him traveling nonstop from studio to studio until he reached the set of Ben Turpin's latest picture. He had been there the day before to apply a black eye to the cross-eyed slapstick comedian's face. He needed to reapply the black eye for a reshoot of the scene. This time, however, tired and flustered, Max made up the wrong eye — and no one noticed. Later, when the studio ran the film, Turpin's black eye jumped from one side to the other. Max couldn't believe he had made such a mistake. The director reassured him. "Don't worry, Max," he said. "We love it. It's great shtick." The scene stayed in the film.

The first of five film versions of Rex Beach's classic novel, *The Spoilers*, was highlighted by a spectacular saloon fistfight be-

Cross-eyed comedian Ben Turpin.

tween actors William Farnum and Tom Santschi, both big, brawny he-men. To ensure the action was as realistic as possible, neither held anything back as the scene was shot, leaving their faces bruised and bloodied. There was little for Max to do to add to the mess.

Young Frank Factor was only ten years old when he first saw *The Spoilers* in 1914, and he remembered telling his school chums that his father had done the frightening make-up for the fight scene. "It was childish pride in my father's make-up skills that wouldn't let me admit that those signs of violence were actually real ones. So I brazenly told my friends that all that facial gore and destruction had been applied by my very own father."

Max had drilled truth and honesty into his children, yet he admitted to repeating Frank's yarn himself. It was too good a bit of promotion to overlook.

By 1916 Max Factor had been in Los Angeles for eight years. He had become a U.S. citizen in 1912. He had made great inroads with the moviemakers and studio heads. His hairpieces and movie make-up were in great demand. He had created other new products that were gaining attention, such as his original Henna Shampoo for theatrical performers and eye shadow and the eyebrow pencil for his yet-to-be announced nontheatrical Society line of make-up. He had coined the word "brownette" for the approximately 50 percent of all women whose hair color ranged between blonde and brunette (the term later fell into disuse). And another son, Sidney, had been added to the family.

Downtown Los Angeles was booming. Max knew it was time to move his store from South Central Avenue. He leased larger space in office-type quarters on the second floor of the prestigious Pantages Building — named after the legendary Alexander Pantages, whose vaudeville house on South Broadway had been instrumental in establishing L.A.'s theater district. With the move, Max Factor was no longer on the edge of downtown. He was at the center of it all.

4

New Directions

Max was proud of his new location. Sometimes he acted as if he'd never had a store on South Central Avenue, as if he'd never had a world of experience leading to this point in his life. He once told a reporter, "I began in a little room in the old Pantages Building in downtown Los Angeles."

There was reason for his pride. He had a store, which would always be called "the store" no matter where it was located, but now he had much more. For the first time in America, perhaps ever, there was a special room, away from the up-front displays and products, where clients were made up: a professional make-up and hairstyling salon. Max still had to travel to the movie studios and various film locations at times, but the stars could now enjoy the privacy and comfort of his salon, with its full mirrors, proper lighting, and more supplies than he could carry in his make-up kit. He had a loyal following.

Ben Turpin credited Max with increasing his popularity when the cosmetician gave him the biggest laugh of his career with the unintentional jumping black eye routine. Turpin was always the first person waiting for Max to open his salon at 5:30 a.m., so he could be in the chair and at work by 7 a.m.

Young Frank Factor would wake at sunrise to see the

gathering crowd, mainly of movie funnymen, outside the store. "It was impossible to keep me away from the place," he remembered, "even though it meant getting up a good three hours before I had to leave for school. Those gatherings of the comics were just too good to miss, every bit as good as a circus."

The scene often turned rowdy. One of Frank's most memorable and spectacular sightings was of Turpin and the equally hilarious Snub Pollard. "First they argued over who would be first to get Father's services, then they came to blows. The fight lasted about a minute and ended in a draw, leaving one of Ben's crossed eyes really black, Snub's lip cut, and the plate glass from one of our biggest supply cases scattered across the floor," Frank recalled. Turpin and Pollard each insisted the other pay for the damage, but Max wouldn't let them; he wanted only to get on with his work. The excitement over, Frank happily went off to school to thrill his classmates with a firsthand account of the fight between two stars they had seen and laughed at onscreen.

Comedians weren't Max's only clients. Mary Pickford and Mary Miles Minter were both young, beautiful actresses, with curly blonde hair. Not only did they share the same first name, but at a glance the two girls very much resembled each other. Pickford had come to California in 1910 with D. W. Griffith's troupe of Biograph players. Minter was ten years younger, but to her aggressive stage mother, Charlotte, Pickford stood in the way of her daughter's success. "They are too much alike," she repeatedly complained to Max. "They have too much in common." She wanted him to turn Pickford into a brunette, but he refused. He had a better idea, which he believed would gain Minter even more attention than her gorgeous curls. Max relaxed her tight curls into softer waves that dipped gently over her forehead and fell past her shoulders. Charlotte wasn't convinced until she saw the new, adult hairstyle he had created especially for her little Mary. It worked. Mary Pickford kept her golden curls, for which she became famous, and Mary Miles Minter went on to become a young sophisticate.

Gloria Swanson was another fan. She entrusted her make-up and hairstyling completely to Max. Having graduated from "bathing beauty" comedies and light, romantic roles to serious dramas, she decided her look needed to reflect that change. For her make-up, Max used several shades darker than she'd worn in her earlier films, with custom eye shadow to heighten the impact of her eyes. For her hair, the change was even more dynamic. Swanson was known for her wild and frizzy style, but Max gave her a short cut, distinctly sleek and severe. She made the transition from comedienne to one of the screen's most popular and glamorous stars, becoming the highest-paid actress in Hollywood in the mid-1920s.

Francis X. Bushman, Wallace Reid, and Harold Lockwood were among the first great matinee idols. As their popularity grew, so did their insecurity. They constantly asked Max if he was giving their rivals special treatment and attention. He tried to convince them that he wasn't favoring one over the other. "Even with all their fame, looks, and talent," Max observed, "they were so uneasy and frightened, like scared peacocks. Sometimes the men are worse than the women." It wasn't just vanity, however — it was business.

And show business was full of interesting characters. The Beery brothers were a popular duo; Wallace played the comedian and Noah the sinister villain. When Noah was cast in a minstrel show, he needed to perform in blackface for the role. Unknown to Noah, his brother had sneaked into his dressing room, emptied the jar of Max's blackface make-up, and filled it with heavy-duty bootblacking.

When Noah finished his first day of shooting and discovered that cleansing cream had no effect on the black polish, he stormed back to see Max, threatened to tear him apart, then, once recovered from his injuries, to take him to court. Surrounded by his children, who quietly witnessed Noah's tirade, Max nervously opened a jar of his black make-up, smeared it all over his face, then easily removed it with cleansing cream. "There, you see," he said, trying to sound calm, "it comes off. Who has been in your jar?"

Noah didn't say a word. He simply stood still for a moment, then he was gone. Max knew Wallace was responsible; Noah had been the victim of his brother's practical jokes many times in the past.

It was almost two months before Noah returned to apologize to Max for his outburst. He admitted he hadn't spoken to his brother since it happened.

In 1917, when Douglas Fairbanks spotted professional wrestler Bull Montana during a match in New York, he persuaded him to go to Los Angeles. "You'll make more money in the movies than you ever will in the ring," Fairbanks told him. The Italian-born Montana arrived in L.A. that same year and never lacked for work, especially after Fairbanks began managing his career.

Cast as a thug and a brute, Montana was one of the most ferocious and sinister-looking villains of all time, despite his actual sweet, gentle manner. "They call me 'mashed-face' and 'plug-ugly,'" he dejectedly told Max. "With your make-up I can look better. You can make me handsome." More than anything, he said, he wanted to be a matinee idol like Douglas Fairbanks and Wallace Reid.

Max studied his features, searching for ways to improve his appearance. The hulking figure had thick black eyebrows, a flattened nose, brutally cauliflowered ears, battle-scarred skin, cracked lips, and excessively puffy eyes. Max knew he could work miracles with make-up, but Bull Montana needed more than make-up to transform his face.

"Do you know why you are so in demand for pictures? Do you know why the public loves you and goes to your movies?" Max said finally. "Because you have a special look. Douglas Fairbanks can't do what you do. Only you the people believe in those roles. I can make you look somewhat better, but what would happen to your career? What you have now will go on and on."

Bull Montana regularly came to see Max after that, not only to be made up for his films but to chat. During his long career he appeared in nearly ninety films.

At the time, the studios did not have make-up departments of their own, so actors had to learn how to apply it themselves or have Max do it for them. That changed in February 1917, with Paramount's *Joan the Woman*, starring Geraldine Farrar. For the first time ever, a script took make-up into consideration, and Max was hired to supervise.

The demands on him were increasing, but he still found time between assignments and clients to work in his lab to devise innovations for the screen, some seemingly frivolous but absolutely vital to the growing complexities of filmmaking. For instance, in comedic sketches, custard pies were often thrown in the actors' faces. The meringue on real pies was too light, and whipped cream was too expensive. Max solved the problem with an oil-based synthetic meringue, which was both cheap and "ploppy" and, most important, stuck to faces without running too quickly.

Phyllis Haver soon tired of pies being thrown in her face. She wanted to move on to dramatic roles in feature films. She turned to Max for help. To enhance her close-ups, he created false eyelashes for her, using human hair. It wasn't long before Haver found her niche as a seductive temptress in melodramas and false eyelashes became all the rage on and off the screen.

It was during this time that Max developed Supreme Liquid Whitener. Though it was originally created as a theatrical product, in 1917 he introduced it as a glamorizing aid for the average woman to achieve flawless alabaster smoothness on her neck, shoulders, arms, and hands. Supreme Liquid Whitener was packaged in a metal can with a dusty pink label featuring Max Factor's image, with the promise, "Will not rub off, contains no lead, is not injurious, and gives the skin a natural color."

On September 2, 1918, Max announced that he had at last completed experiments on his Color Harmony line, created for

Max Factor first created false eyelashes for Phyllis Haver.

the screen. It was his belief that certain combinations of natural skin, hair, and eye colors were most effectively complemented by specific make-up shades. Until then, there were only three shades of face powder available for all complexions: white, pink, and flesh. Max developed eleven precisely graduated shades, a range wide enough to harmonize with many skin colors.

As Max worked in his lab testing color tones for the entire make-up range, son Frank distributed samples of the powders to the girls at school, without letting on that they were test subjects.

"I got it from the store just for you," he would say. Frank dutifully noted their responses to the new product for his father.

Max had done his own secret testing, using screen sirens Nita Naldi and Carmel Myers. The two stars were thrilled to be working with him and honored to be among the first to try his new Color Harmony line. He later credited their vocal and unceasing endorsements for the quick acceptance of his new products by local shops.

Max's principle of Color Harmony soon ensured more predictable and desirable results on film. It was a revolutionary concept, one he hoped would one day convince masses of women, not only in Hollywood but worldwide, that there was nothing inherently sinful in embellishing their natural physical gifts.

With more innovations in development and production, the business was quickly running out of room in the Pantages Building. He rented warehouse space on nearby Brooklyn Avenue, but even that wasn't enough. He soon found it necessary to move the store again, this time to 326 South Hill Street. He was back on street level, with splashy, in-your-face signs promoting his various products and services. A large retractable awning trumpeted his name, and along the side of the store, stretching from the ground floor to the second, was the boldest sign of all: "The House of Make-Up."

In the past, Max had to announce a change of location. Not anymore. The stars and the studios knew his every move; his services had become invaluable to them. Most of his customers also turned to him for friendship; he was a trusted confidant and father figure. They called him "Pops," and he called them by their real names, even if they had become famous under a pseudonym. They poured out their most intimate thoughts, problems, and secrets as they sat in his chair, sometimes for hours, while he created a new look or hairstyle — and listened. His celebrity clients learned some of his secrets, too — beauty secrets that would make them unforgettable to the moviegoing public. The store at

326 South Hill Street quickly became the rendezvous for all the players of the silent screen and the fast-growing film community. Max once commented, "During the years of my work I have enjoyed friendships with stars from the earliest days on, friendships that are worth more to me than anything else in the world."

Rudolph Valentino first came to see Max in 1920, using the name Rudolf Valentine, which had been given him a few years earlier when he began appearing in films. The young, Italian-born

Max Factor's House of Make-Up on South Hill Street
in downtown Los Angeles, 1920.

Rodolfo Alfonzo Raffaelo Pierre Filibert Guglielmi de Valentina d'Antonguolla, had made his living as a waiter, gigolo, and café dancer before arriving in the United States in 1913. In New York he was a taxi dancer and Broadway performer before becoming involved in a scandal with a wealthy married woman.

In 1917 he found himself in Los Angeles, where he landed bit parts in films as handsome but sleazy gangsters and villains. But he was not a happy man. As he admitted in his 1922 "auto-biography" published in *Movie Weekly*, "I was selected for villains because of my dark complexion and somewhat foreign aspect, I presume. This was a cause of regret for me, for I realized that the 'heavy' has usually a slight chance of attaining the most profitable and desirable positions in motion picture acting."

Valentino's chance to leave his villainous parts behind came in the role of a lifetime, the lead in Rex Ingram's production of *The Four Horsemen of the Apocalypse*. He was given a screen test, but failed. To mask the darkness of his skin, he had made himself up with a light shade of pink greasepaint, which photographed as ghastly white. But Ingram was willing to give Valentino another chance, and Max was called to work with him.

Valentino presented more problems than the coloring of his skin. He had a scar on his right cheek. His eyebrows were too heavy, his hair unruly. And he was overweight. While all of these issues could be corrected, Max's biggest challenge remained to create a make-up shade to complement Valentino's complexion, one that wouldn't make him look cadaverous onscreen.

In those days, before shade-sensitive Panchromatic film, cre-ating the perfect make-up for Valentino was no easy task. According to notes in the Factor archives, "It took several days of painstaking experiment and testing, during which Valentino, aware that his whole future in films might depend upon the suc-cess of this effort, established a steady daytime residence in our studio. Sitting on a workbench, he would quietly watch Max's ac-tivities for hours on end, frequently breaking the silence by ask-ing, 'Any luck, Max?' Finally, the constant pestering got on Max's nerves, so he put Rudolph to work mixing pigment and grinding his own make-up, which he did willingly and well."

Eventually, Max came up with what he believed to be the correct coloring, a dark yellow greasepaint, and Rex Ingram was called in. "Not that! Not THAT!" Ingram cried. "Do you want him to look like the end man in a minstrel show? He's too dark as it is."

"Yes," Max replied politely, tilting Valentino's chin and streaking it with dark yellow. He added deft touches to his lips and delicate shading around his nose, and trimmed his eyebrows. Then he stood back. "Try him now," Max said.

The subsequent black-and-white screen tests, with the addition of longer sideburns and a dollop of Max's product, Brillox, to slick back his hair, captured for the first time the look that made female hearts flutter and Rudolph Valentino a major star.

In 1923 America's first imported star came in the person of Pola Negri, who had signed a contract with Paramount. A huge success in German films, she was famous for her exotic appearance and for playing passionate women of mystery. No sooner had she arrived at the studio than she was taken to Max's Hill Street salon.

He had looked forward to meeting Paramount's newest actress, mainly because she was Polish, but no one had warned him about her temper. Only moments after he began working on her, she started screaming. He couldn't imagine what he was doing to upset her. Everything, apparently! She complained about his way of applying make-up; it was not what she had been accustomed to in Europe. She screamed, first in English, then in Polish, and threatened to throw things. Normally a quiet and patient man, Max refused to tolerate her outburst. Suddenly he roared back at her in her native tongue, and promised to throw even larger objects if she didn't behave. Pola Negri was instantly silenced. A smile crossed her face and she began to laugh. Max looked at her sternly, then he too began to laugh. From then on, she was cooperative whenever he worked with her. She returned frequently to the salon, and they ultimately became close friends.

Wallace, the Beery family comedian, wasn't so amusing to Max when he arrived to be made up for his role in *The Lost World*. Although he strongly objected to wearing make-up, he and Max somehow managed to remain friends over the years, even as he sat in the make-up chair mumbling and grumbling. This time, however, it was Wallace's hair that brought on his fussing. His role in the new film required large ringlets, which prompted a tirade of cursing and references to Little Lord Fauntleroy and Peter Pan. He refused to appear "foppish" in the film, he insisted.

Max was used to working with difficult subjects. He made a call to the studio, then put Wallace on the line. After a few minutes, the actor calmed down enough for Max to turn his once straight hair into a curly mop, and filming proceeded as scheduled.

5

The Roaring Twenties

The word "make-up" was taboo in polite society. It was a word used in the theater by actors and other entertainers thought to be of dubious reputations. It had a vulgar connotation and conjured images of painted faces and a permissive, bohemian way of life. During these post-Victorian times, women had no objection to the genteel use of "cosmetics" — a little powder and a hint of lip pomade, perhaps — but they would have been shocked if anyone referred to these as "make-up."

Max believed that the new art of make-up, with its quality ingredients, innovative, precise techniques, and high artistic standards — which could never have been possible without the testing ground of theater and motion pictures — had earned the right to be called by its own name. But he was hesitant about presenting the products he had developed using a term regarded by many as risqué.

Frank Factor, younger and less bound by tradition, argued that his father's make-up presented merits that were never known or even heard of before. It was time to break away and start a new tradition, he reasoned. On July 9, 1920, Max gave in to his son and officially began referring to his beautifying products as "make-up." The new term caught on and found favor worldwide, even among manufacturers who had long avoided even hinting at the word on their labels, product literature, or advertising.

One day in 1922 Max announced to Davis and Frank, "I'm taking your mother on vacation." They would be in Europe for several weeks, and he instructed his sons to run the store in his absence. He had rarely taken time off, and never a vacation, so the news came as quite a surprise to the boys. "We were worried at first," Davis later admitted, "because there were so many new responsibilities we knew nothing about. But once we were on our own, we worked harder than ever to show Father how well we could do by ourselves."

While Max and Jennie were in Germany, he decided to visit the offices of Leichner, which he had long represented in the United States as the company's top retailer of their theatrical stick greasepaint. It was time, he had decided, to ask for a larger commission on his sales of their products.

When he introduced himself at the front desk, he expected to be greeted warmly. Instead, he was told to sit and wait. Ignored for more than an hour, Max grew increasingly angry. He stormed out of Leichner, hurried back to his hotel, and cabled his sons. "Start selling greasepaint in tubes," it read. Only five words, but it wasn't long before Leichner felt their impact.

Max had long experimented with the idea of selling greasepaint in collapsible tubes, believing them to be more convenient and hygienic than the stick form, which was often messy and difficult to use. He stocked his own brand in jars, but his newest creation in tubes was a completely different type of smooth, creamy greasepaint that could be applied more thinly and evenly, and provided even better results than his original greasepaint in jars.

Created in thirty-one shades from White, Very Light Pink, and Sallow to Sunburn, Dark Brown, and Black, each numbered in the series, the new greasepaint was packaged in Kelly green tubes. A message from Max Factor, over his signature, read, "After years of study in the art of make-up, I claim to have perfected the highest standard of greasepaint. The ingredients contained herein are of the highest quality, thus making this preparation superior to all others. The advantages of this form of greasepaint over the old stick form will be readily realized after once used."

Max had made no attempt to market his own greasepaint while he was handling other brands. He especially respected his long association with Leichner, which enjoyed strong brand recognition and loyalty among theatrical performers at the time. The cool reception he had received at Leichner headquarters in Germany, intentional or not, resulted in the launching of the world's first "sanitary" make-up. Before long, Max Factor's brand of greasepaint was outselling both Leichner and Minor combined, making it the number one brand on the market.

Max had another reason to be delighted following his return from Europe: the sterling performance of his two sons. The business had not only survived, it had thrived. Since his earliest days in Los Angeles, when he opened his first store, he had envisioned a family business. Now, a dozen years later, he decided the time had come for his two oldest sons to assume major responsibilities, full-time.

Davis, at twenty-two, was a natural businessman with true leadership abilities, and was named general manager. Frank, nearly twenty, was not only working in the lab with his father and exhibiting some talent as a perfumer, he was spending time as a "field test man" for the Color Harmony line. And on what better faces than Mary Pickford, Mabel Normand, Lillian and Dorothy Gish, and Colleen Moore for him to gain experience as a make-up artist?

Not all of Frank's experience during his training came from working with the ladies of the screen, however. One of his more unforgettable encounters took place when he was "doing regular uncomplicated motion picture applications" for his father and the rugged actor Jack Holt came into the salon needing immediate attention. Holt was not alone. Walking by his side was one of the big names of the movies, the German shepherd Rin Tin Tin, who had been rescued from a bombed-out kennel in France during

World War I and brought to the United States, where he became a canine star.

Rin Tin Tin and Holt were appearing in a film together, and were very close. The dog never let Holt out of his sight, possibly because the actor kept tossing him bits of a chocolate bar. As Frank remembered, "The dog star was handily nearby when I stepped in to smooth make-up over Holt's face. Then, either because he didn't know me, or because he didn't quite approve of me, or maybe because he mistook the make-up procedures for something sinister, he came to the rescue of his pal Holt by biting me on the calf of my right leg. Once again, I suffered for the sake of my art." From then on, whenever Frank knew he was going to be around Rin Tin Tin, he made sure he brought a stash of chocolate with him.

As for the other two boys, they would eventually have important leadership roles in the company. For now, however, fifteen-year-old Louis worked in the Hill Street store and made deliveries after school. Sidney, not yet in his teens, concentrated only on his schoolwork.

By 1922 Max had his eye on the growing Jewish community of Boyle Heights in East Los Angeles. He had no plans to again move the store; this time it was his family. They had relocated every time the shop changed addresses, and usually to less-than-spacious quarters adjacent to the business, or above it, on the busy streets of Los Angeles. Now he wanted his family to have a real home.

Boyle Heights was near the store, only several miles away. There, Max found a two-story, 3,100-square-foot Craftsman-style house, built in 1907, on a quiet residential street. It had four large bedrooms, separate dining room, maid's room, laundry chute, two east-facing solariums, one on each floor, with rich wood paneling throughout, and a large garage where he set up a small lab. Today the house is still a jewel, preserved to retain its historic elegance, along with decorative features, including imported crystal wall sconces installed by Max himself.

The Factor home in Boyle Heights, ca. 1990s.

The completion of the move to his new home and the greater involvement of his sons in the business allowed Max to focus on his clients. More than any other male star, Douglas Fairbanks continually needed his services. Fairbanks's tough, fast-growing beard had to be shaved in the morning before he left for the set, then again in the middle of the day, requiring his make-up to be removed and reapplied. If filming continued deep into the night, as was often necessary, he had to be shaved and made up a third, sometimes a fourth, time. But it was his 1924 film *The Thief of Baghdad*, a stunt-filled Arabian Nights fantasy, that had the actor requesting Max's special attention. Fairbanks was famous for his daring athletic feats: jumping, swinging, climbing, and tumbling over set pieces. His new movie had him doing all that and more, such as leaping in and out of enormous jugs. He needed body make-up that was resistant to perspiration and that wouldn't smear on props, costumes, and scenery during his physical sequences. Max rose to the challenge and created the first perspiration-proof body make-up that would not rub off under any and all rigorous conditions. Then he devised the reverse — cinematic sweat — by simply combining equals parts of water with mineral oil. When shaken violently and sprayed on the skin, it was possible to achieve everything from the look of a "nervous sweat" to a very convincing "hardworking man's sweat."

The following year the Factors received their largest single order of body make-up to date: more than six hundred gallons of a light olive shade for MGM's epic *Ben-Hur*, and it was needed "on the double." The rush order was necessary because filming, most of which had been done in Italy, was being completed at the studio in Culver City, and the skin of the thousands of newly hired extras was much lighter than that of the original Italian extras. MGM was concerned that audiences would notice the variance in skin tones, unduly affecting critical response to the spectacular production, which cost a then record $4 million. According to the Factor files, "By ordering all other activities in our laboratories stopped, we managed to get out the needed six hundred gallons of make-up and delivered to the studio in less than two hours."

Another MGM rush order for body make-up came for the underwater scenes in the 1926 World War I spy film *Mare Nostrum*. This time, however, the make-up needed by the studio did not exist, prompting Max to head to his lab, with Frank at his side. The Factors worked for six straight days and nights, sleeping in the lab rather than taking the time to go home. A new formula that totally resisted water had to be found. It didn't help, Frank later reported, that producer-director Rex Ingram called at hourly intervals, concerned that a waterproof formula could not be concocted. Without the make-up, his film could not be completed. Ingram grew increasingly frantic as he waited and the film's expensive financial overhead mounted.

The good news came on the seventh day. The Factors had successfully formulated and tested a new completely waterproof make-up! The product was so effective, it continued to be used in hundreds of productions, including the popular Esther Williams aquatic musicals of the 1940s and '50s. It also became the basis for Max Factor's retail collection of waterproof make-up for face, cheeks, and eyes, which was introduced to the general public in 1971.

Max Factor's waterproof make-up, modeled by Cristina Ferrare.

The Roaring Twenties saw the rise of the "siren" female lead — daring, exotic actresses who tested the boundaries of film censorship. Young women everywhere began discarding staid old Victorian traditions for independence, faster living, and flashier looks and styles. Max, who always had his finger on the pulse, wanted to design a bold new look for lips.

He had built a solid reputation within the motion picture industry as a reliable and creative problem-solver. But although he had responded to virtually every challenge presented to him by the stars and the studios, he was continually frustrated by one vexing problem: under the hot lights necessary for filming, lip pomade melted off the actresses' mouths and ran into their greasepaint foundation.

Following much experimentation, the technique he finally devised couldn't have been more simple. After applying the greasepaint, which camouflaged the existing outlines of the mouth, he dipped his thumb into the pomade and pressed two thumbprints onto the upper lip. Then he turned his thumb upside down and pressed another thumbprint onto the center of the lower lip. Finally, he used a brush to contour the lip.

Max Factor's "bee-stung lips," first worn by actress Mae Murray, was a puckered, kissable, daring look that captured the spirit of the '20s. Bee-stung lips were also known as "vampire lips" and "rosebud lips," depending on whether the actresses were playing vamps or romantic roles. Before the decade was over, however, technical advances in filmmaking forced Max to create a completely new line of make-up for the movies, and with it, the ability to fully draw lips to the corners of an actress's mouth.

As Max's fame spread outside the film community, more and more newspapers and magazines requested interviews with the master of make-up. He had been interviewed many times before, but he spoke poorly and in broken English, so he was often misunderstood and frequently misquoted.

The family decided he would no longer talk to the press. In the early 1930s, once the company had grown large enough for

Mae Murray in full hair and make-up.

an in-house public relations department, all interviews were handled by department head Len Smith. Some of the information released was incorrect and glamorized, similar to what the studios were handing out about their stars, but the pressure was off Max, freeing him to practice his craft. His most important work was yet to come.

6

Recognition and Growth

s more and more young women sat in darkened theaters thinking Clara Bow's bee-stung lips and Theda Bara's daring rouge and shocking mascara looked irresistible, they began testing the limits of old-fashioned respectability. Worse, the immoral word "make-up" had replaced the more refined and acceptable "cosmetics," triggering widespread unrest and controversy. Husbands, scandalized by their wives' "tarty new looks," filed for divorce. Horrified parents locked rebellious daughters in their rooms. A bill introduced in the Kansas legislature threatened to make it a misdemeanor for any woman under the age of forty-four to wear cosmetics "for the purpose of creating a false impression." Even Pope Pius XI denounced such "devil's work." It was a losing battle. Make-up madness, like movie madness, was here to stay. The right to rouge was seen as a symbol of freedom from Victorian repression.

Max wanted no part of the controversy and refused comment. He concentrated on his work with the stars, which had its own challenges. When he first met young Colleen Moore, he didn't know what to do with her. Her eyes were of different colors — one was brown, the other blue — which made them

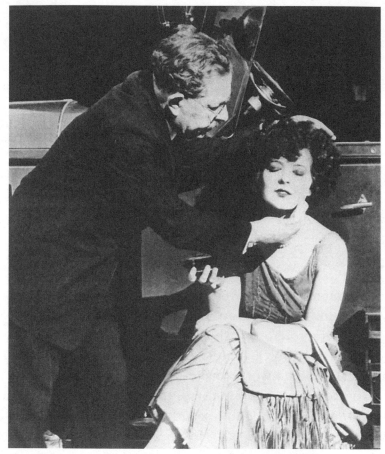

"It Girl" Clara Bow sits on the running board of a car as Max Factor puts the finishing touches to her make-up.

appear light and dark onscreen. Contact lenses hadn't yet been invented, so Colleen's eyes presented a perplexing conundrum. Make-up couldn't change the conflicting colors, so Max created a new hairstyle, one so unusual that the audience's attention would be diverted from her eyes. The Dutch bob was perky, carefree, and brilliantly lustrous. Colleen Moore's "flapper" cut became a trademark of the times, the rage of wannabe "jazz babies" everywhere, and her eyes were a forgotten distraction.

Norma Shearer, who had earlier been rejected by Florenz Ziegfeld as being too short, having fat legs, and a cast in one eye, was sent to Max to "enhance her image" after signing a five-year contract with MGM. Max knew he couldn't do anything with her height or her legs, so he attempted to draw attention from her weak eye with a deeply marcelled fingerwave. Shearer's new hairstyle didn't start a national craze, but it became her signature throughout her career as "the First Lady of MGM."

Greta Garbo's eyes weren't a problem; they were one of her biggest assets. The Swedish-born actress was sent to Max prior to her first American screen test. His verdict? "She has natural eyelashes more lovely than any artificial lashes I can supply." Garbo's luminous eyes captivated the nation. Wrote one critic shortly after her American movie debut in 1926's *The Torrent*, "Until the appearance of those luscious Garbo close-ups, heavy lidded and languorous, our girls never paid attention to their eyes, save for winking and ogling purposes. And suddenly the country has discovered the paramount importance of assisting Nature with the normal eye. Even our nicest people have begun to use mascara and eye shadow. A few years ago, any woman using those devil's tricks would have been called 'fast' and cut dead by the minister's wife. Now, thanks to this seductive Scandinavian, nice women are addressing their eyes, especially for evening wear, and are still received at the parsonage." The critic could have thanked Max, too, for as lovely and beguiling as Garbo's eyes were, Max had made them even more attractive by subtly enhancing them with his make-up.

Max once noted that small eyes could be sexy and big eyes could be innocent, but even he couldn't help a bad nose or teeth. That wasn't entirely true. He contoured and reshaped noses with make-up, and whitened teeth with his tooth enamel, which came in three shades and temporarily concealed discolorations, fillings, and any other visible imperfections. In the days before commercial and professional teeth-whitening products, "More stars than you can imagine had to have the make-up artist paint their teeth," confirmed Frank Factor. Max also created a black tooth enamel to mimic the look of a missing tooth or teeth, if required by a scene.

Max worked overtime to keep the stars and studios happy, but his children had a much grander vision for the future. Although he felt he had all the business he could handle, his two older boys, in particular, convinced him that they should strive to grow the enterprise. Had it not been for them, Max Factor and Company might never have become the global player it did.

Max had recently acquired a nearby building, which he had leased to another company. When the lease expired and the tenants chose not to renew, some of the manufacturing equipment was moved there. Max bought larger powder mills and electrically operated grinding machines, and enlarged the staff. He hired some of Davis's and Frank's former schoolmates, as well as others in the neighborhood, some of whom remained with the company all of their working lives.

To publicize the Factor name, Max did a series of demonstrations around town, in busy theater lobbies, shops, and department stores, and on Sunday afternoons on the popular pier at Venice Beach, which attracted huge crowds of fun-seekers with its rides, restaurants, and ballrooms. Posters went up in Los Angeles and surrounding beach communities announcing, "Make-up contests with motion picture star judges . . . Beauty favors for every entrant . . . And free cases of Max Factor Society Cosmetics."

Max was eager to meet the public and promote his make-up, but he was even more interested in showing women how to correctly apply it. Younger women had no one to teach them because their mothers and grandmothers wore little or no make-up. If the stars needed help, so did the average woman, and that concerned him. As Max demonstrated before the crowds, he shared some of his beauty tips, which appeared in the daily papers following his appearances. Here are a few:

- Don't use make-up that shows. No make-up is good make-up unless the other fellow doesn't know you have it on.

- No beauty or complexion can surmount a skin not properly cleansed. A clean skin is the foundation on which beauty is built. Girls should learn to keep their faces clean with good cream, and not paint themselves up like circus clowns.

- Greasepaint is not for the street. Young girls might use a little powder and a little rouge, if too pale, but only enough to make them look like they had no rouge.

Once Max ended his promotional appearances, several of his personally trained make-up artists replaced him. Following Ruth Gordon's two-day stint at a Pasadena department store, she was quoted as saying, "Every cosmetic, if applied properly, should add to one's appearance and charm. The proper application is the secret. Everything about the face should be considered in order to obtain complete harmony and beauty. And at all times, make-up should be used sparingly rather than in large quantities. When used correctly, make-up should not be noticeable."

These appearances for Max Factor products came to the attention of Sales Builders, Inc., an established company responsible for the advertising, distribution, and sales of a number of products in the United States. Following several weeks of negotiations, Sales Builders signed up Max Factor and Company.

The three owners of Sales Builders — Hess Kramer, Harry Mier, and Joseph Conrad — wasted no time in getting to work. Within days they were doing market research, posing as clerks behind drugstore counters to find out what appealed to women. They told the Factors that the druggist already has the confidence of women because he fills their medical prescriptions, and they rely on him for advice about almost everything they buy in his drugstore. If they could figure out how to get him to recommend Max Factor make-up to them, they would buy it with the same confidence.

Sales Builders quickly recognized a buying pattern among women: most bought one brand of face powder, another of rouge, and still another of lip pomade or lipstick. The goal was to get them to buy all three products from Max Factor. Sales Builders used Max's already established Color Harmony principle to develop the world's first Color Harmony Prescription Make-Up Chart. The chart recommended combinations of powder, rouge, and lipstick in specific shades that worked together to complement every combination of complexion, hair, and eye coloring. Accompanied by the Complexion Analysis Card, it worked like a charm.

Although cosmetics might have been the last thing on a woman's mind when she entered the store, that changed when her druggist or clerk handed her a little card listing the various colors of complexion, hair, and eyes. All she had to do was check off the colors that corresponded to her own, then the clerk would refer to the master chart to show her the appropriate shades of powder, rouge, and lipstick to best complement and enhance her individual coloring. That information was then transferred to her personal Color Harmony Prescription Make-Up Chart, giving her a record of the right shades for her type, which she could refer to easily the next time she needed make-up. The result was a companion sale of three products instead of one, and Max Factor became a hot line. The Color Harmony concept was arguably "the single most important development ever known to the art of make-up."

Sales Builders also armed their salesmen with a special introduction that not only enabled them to physically get a foot in the door but also to open new accounts with a sizable order. It was a short but important sentence, directed to the druggist-owner of the store, which had to be memorized word for word: "We are the people who make, teach, and prescribe all the make-up used by all the stars of motion pictures." The salesmen brought a poster with glowing testimonials from such favorites as

Clara Bow, Laura La Plante, Vilma Bánky, Belle Bennett, Billie Dove, Esther Ralston, and Madge Bellamy, which was later displayed prominently in the store. The ingenious marketing campaign gave Max Factor instant name recognition.

National distribution of Max Factor make-up in October 1927 coincided with the Hollywood premiere of the world's first "talkie" feature, *The Jazz Singer.* The Factor family and everyone who was anyone in the film industry were in attendance. Max knew that bringing sound to the movies would revolutionize film-making, but he had not foreseen that it would affect the art of make-up.

Max had worked with Al Jolson, the star of *The Jazz Singer*, on an experimental sound short, *April Showers*, the previous year. The black greasepaint make-up Jolson had used throughout his highly successful career onstage as "the master showman" in vaudeville wasn't working on film. After experimenting with various greasepaints, Max settled for the make-up used during the earliest of minstrel shows: burnt cork.

The coming of sound also forced changes in lighting and film stock. Because the microphones used for the new movies picked up the noisy sputter of the carbon arc lights — the standard film lighting used for illuminating movie sets and faces for fifteen years — they were substituted with noiseless tungsten lamps, the giant counterparts of the electric light bulb. The new lamps were quiet, but they were much hotter, and banks of them were necessary. They also provided a softer light. The old Orthochromatic film, which had been used since the birth of the film industry, was not sensitive enough to properly record faces under the new lighting.

The old film was replaced by super-sensitive, faster Panchromatic film, but it made faces appear noticeably darker, as if in shadow. The new film made every item in the Max Factor make-up line for motion pictures instantly obsolete.

It took nearly six months for Max and Frank to test and perfect an entirely new formulation in a wider-than-ever range of shades that reflected the correct degree of light required by the sensitive new film. It had only one drawback. Because it was designed for black-and-white film, it looked bizarre in real life. For example, actresses wore dark brown lipstick, which photographed as red on film. The new line was impossible to wear as everyday make-up and "horrifying to look at," Frank admitted.

Max Factor's Panchromatic make-up brought him accolades. At the first annual Mardi Gras Ball, hosted by the newly formed Motion Pictures Make-Up Artists' Association, a group consisting primarily of Factor-trained make-up artists, he received a plaque of appreciation signed by movie stars, film executives, and make-up artists.

From George Westmore, director of MGM's make-up department, came this personal note: "In our talking pictures, the question of make-up becomes even a more vital issue than ever before, and I have found in using your make-up I have always been able to obtain the best results. . . . Perfect results in photography and reliability are the two important reasons we use your make-up exclusively in our studio."

On April 30, 1928, Max Factor was presented with a special certificate by the Academy of Motion Picture Arts and Sciences, the very first awarded by the academy, in recognition of his contribution to the success of "Incandescent Illumination Research." Frank remembered, "I had never seen my father simultaneously so happy and so on the verge of tears. He just said 'Thank you' and sat down, for he wasn't able to speak. And he told me years later, that he considered that occasion, when the entire motion picture industry gathered to pay him tribute for his achievements in the cosmetic art, to be the happiest moment of his life." (It wasn't until 1981 that make-up became a regular category of the Academy Awards.)

Max Factor's Panchromatic make-up was trademarked on October 11, 1929. As his reputation scaled new heights, virtually every part of his company was expanding. The Hill Street address had served him well, but the business had outgrown that location years earlier, forcing him to lease additional properties on the periphery of downtown Los Angeles. It was important to gather all the pieces together in one location. And there was only one logical choice — Hollywood.

7

Hollywood

*E*arly in 1915, while John Barrymore was scouting a hilltop home in the heights above Hollywood, he reportedly commented as he looked across the scraggly landscape, "My God, almost anything we do here will be an improvement."

Although Hollywood was incorporated as a city in 1903, it never had its own mayor, city hall, divorce court, or even civic center. It was merely a designated suburb, annexed to Los Angeles in 1910. Its prominence was based on the influx of movie studios that located there.

The Hollywood of 1928 was no longer the sleepy farmland community Max had seen in 1913 when he visited Cecil B. DeMille at the barn where *The Squaw Man* was being filmed. Gone were the orange groves and pepper trees that lined the dusty flatlands. The main street that ran through town, known then as Prospect Avenue, had been renamed Hollywood Boulevard and was bustling with fancy cars and foot traffic, many of whom were locals and newcomers walking the street in picture make-up, whether or not they were in the movies. Opulent theaters with exotic forecourts and names, such as the Egyptian and the Chinese, run by showman Sid Grauman, were filled with moviegoers. Commercial buildings, restaurants, banks, and hotels had risen between the remaining Queen Anne, Victorian, and Mission Revival residences. There were motion picture studios, churches, and a library. And in the hills just to the north, an enormous sign spelled out HOLLYWOODLAND, promoting a new housing development.

Near the corner of Hollywood Boulevard and Highland Avenue, diagonally across the street from the famed Hollywood Hotel, the favorite meeting place of the big-name luminaries of the day, stood an abandoned four-story building that was formerly home to the Hollywood Storage Company. It also contained a huge basement that once housed a bowling alley, plus a mammoth freight elevator in the back. Built in 1914, the building had seen better days, but it offered everything Max could possibly need: space, a great location, and ample room for expansion.

He bought the building in early 1928, and on March 22, just sixteen days after the close of escrow, a ceremony was held to dedicate the new cornerstone. Actress Thelma Hill, a former Mack Sennett bathing beauty who had appeared in silent comedies with Ben Turpin and Laurel and Hardy, christened the cornerstone with a bottle of Max Factor's Skin Freshener rather than champagne, which brought scattered chuckles from the onlookers. A massive renovation of the building was already on the drawing board, and as work began on April 1, banners lined Hollywood Boulevard to welcome Max Factor to the community.

Max wanted to make the building as functionally modern as possible and visually magnificent in every way, capturing both the glamour of Hollywood and the elegance of royalty, which he recalled from his early days in the palaces of Russia. The grand salon, in particular, had to make an immediate impression on everyone who entered his newest "store," whether it was the stars of motion pictures or the nonprofessional women who simply wandered in from the street.

The finished result met his lofty goals. The palatial salon was in the style of Louis XIV. Designed in muted jewel tones with gold and bronze accents, it was grand in every way. The walls of the octagonal room were lined with mirrors and topped with curved friezes dedicated to the vanities of the day: music, opera, dance, and motion pictures. Gorgeous imported crystal chandeliers hung from coffered ceilings. Trompe l'oeil details separated recessed, illuminated wall displays, while prismatic glass showcases held everything from perfumes and cosmetics to powder puffs, hairpieces, and false eyelashes. Underfoot was beautiful parquet flooring.

One showcase featured custom make-up cases. The most expensive — covered in patent leather and filled with exquisite combs and brushes, cut-glass perfume spray bottles, plate glass mirrors, and glittering accessories — were favored by Hollywood newcomers who seemed to believe these would help them break into show business. In reality, as Max or his assistants would attest, the bigger the star, the less impressive the make-up kit. John Barrymore carried his essentials on a twenty-five-cent tray. Phyllis Haver used a ten-cent wicker basket. Douglas Fairbanks kept his in a battered folding table. Lon Chaney, a make-up master himself, used an old satchel that contained "everything but the proverbial kitchen sink."

Adjoining the salon was the make-up and consultation room. One of the newspaper reporters who previewed the new Factor location made special mention that this room was "entirely in hygienic white, with revolving chairs, where the screen or stage actor sits before specially regulated mirrors under exactly the same lighting conditions obtained from Klieg lights, before the footlights, or in bright sunshine or gleaming chandeliers of a ballroom."

A small section of the wig department, also on the main floor, had another mirrored, specially lighted "fitting room," where wigs were tried on and adjusted from all angles. Featureless wooden heads, many donned in wigs, lined several walls.

Upstairs was the new product and development laboratory. Adjacent to Max's lab was the perfumery, which had over two thousand containers of various scents, oils, and colorings. Two particularly valuable vials caught a reporter's attention. One held the essence of mogra, a flower from India "which lives but a day and dies," and the other, the essence of rare Alpine rose.

In one of the bright, sunny upstairs rooms, reporters also found numerous jars of creams, tubes of greasepaint, lotions, and powders in a rainbow of shades, all being manufactured, labeled, and boxed. Wrote one, "I saw a great vat, containing fifty gallons of boiling liquid turn right before my eyes into a whipped cream substance, and immediately thereafter into solidified cold cream. It was poured onto great steam rollers, came out as smooth as butter, and before you could say Jack Robinson was being pressed into tubes by uncanny machinery as you ever saw go around."

Also on the second floor were the general offices and a clubroom, which Max made available each week to members of the Motion Picture Make-Up Artists' Association for discussions and make-up demonstrations. If any member had problems with a current or forthcoming production, Max was there to help. On the top floor was the main wig department, along with an assembly line for packaging and loading merchandise onto the freight elevator.

The grand opening of the new Max Factor building was held on Saturday night, November 17, 1928. As Max walked through the front door following the ribbon-cutting, he said, "When I think of my first little store in Los Angeles, it seems like a dream come true to enter this building." Once inside, he welcomed guests to his new flower-filled showroom and posed for photos. Passersby that day, and in the years to come, marveled at his magnificent display windows along Highland Avenue. There were five celebrity-themed windows, which became the hallmarks of the new Max Factor headquarters.

Shortly after the opening, in early 1929, Max was called to make up over two thousand extras for the flood scene in *Noah's Ark*. It was a rush request for waterproof make-up, which had to be applied in less than two hours, before the day's shooting began. Although Max had personally trained over forty make-up artists to handle studio requirements, few could be called in from assignments, especially on such short notice, and the process of doing full-body make-up was a lengthy one.

Under serious time pressure, Max and Frank hit upon the idea of using airbrushes to spray the make-up on the thousands of extras. Adding a liquid solvent to the make-up rendered it fluid enough to be sprayed, in much the same way car manufacturers lacquered motor cars. As Frank recalled, "It was like sending them through a car wash." However, the stars and featured players who required close-ups still had to be carefully and individually made up. Among the extras in the flood scene were two then unknowns, Andy Devine and John Wayne.

On October 29, 1929, also known as Black Tuesday, the stock market crash sent America, and the world, reeling. Hundreds of banks closed within the first month. Massive layoffs followed, leaving millions of people penniless, jobless, and homeless.

As the world sank deeper into the Great Depression, Hollywood survived. People sought a few hours of escape at the movies where, for only a few pennies, they could see exotic locations, beautiful costumes, and glamorous, smiling faces. Frank said of the company business at that time, "It remained remarkably sound."

Max often took time to help some of the less fortunate on his way to work each day. He was driven by Louis in the big company Town Car, which otherwise sat covered with a tarp in the Boyle Heights driveway, since he used the garage as his at-home lab. Max would ask Louis to pull up to the curb so he could get out and hand money to strangers. If he took a bus to work, which he preferred because he loved being around people, he'd get off to hand out dollar bills, then get back on again. Many of Max's client friends did what they could to help, too. Marion Davies and Al Jolson were among the celebrities who periodically served in Hollywood soup kitchens that fed the unemployed.

In lieu of expensive newspaper and magazine advertising, the Factors continued to schedule make-up demonstrations in movie theater lobbies, believing that their products were priced within the reach of anyone who could afford to buy a movie ticket. They offered female moviegoers a free make-up application in the special booth in the lobby. "Try Max Factor's famous cosmetics of the stars and see how lovely you really can look," read one of the posters. Many bought on the spot, not just one or two items but all the products that were used in their respective demonstrations.

Advertising was on the horizon for the Factors. Max had long been proud of his strong association and friendships with the stars, particularly the leading ladies of the screen. Sales Builders came up with the idea of using celebrity endorsements in Max Factor advertising. Arrangements were made with the stars through their studios. In return, Max Factor would promote the stars' latest films — all for the grand sum of one dollar, if the stars were willing, an arrangement that would cost millions today. Among the celebrities to team up with Max Factor were such luminaries as Jean Arthur, Mary Astor, Lucille Ball, Joan Bennett, Madeleine Carroll, Joan Crawford, Frances Dee, Ellen Drew, Irene Dunne, Joan Fontaine, Paulette Goddard, Betty Grable, Rita Hayworth, Miriam Hopkins, Marsha Hunt, Veronica Lake, Hedy Lamarr, Myrna Loy, Ida Lupino, Ann Miller, Patricia Morison, Anna Neagle, Merle Oberon, Maureen O'Hara, Maureen O'Sullivan, Gail Patrick, Rosalind Russell, Ann Rutherford, Anne Shirley, Penny Singleton, Ann Sothern, Barbara Stanwyck, Margaret Sullivan, Lana Turner, and Loretta Young. By the 1950s virtually every major actress and aspiring starlet had signed on to be a Max Factor Girl. The fabulous faces of the stars were living testimonials to Max Factor's revolutionary new make-up.

During the Depression, Max's biggest rivals were two female entrepreneurs who had also launched their businesses around the turn of the century. Helena Rubinstein, like Max, had been born in Poland. Elizabeth Arden was born in Canada, and, like Rubinstein, began by operating beauty salons. Both women emphasized the importance of skin care and were keenly aware of how effective luxurious packaging could be. Rubinstein believed, "There are no ugly women, only lazy ones." Arden had a more subtle approach, stressing, "Hold fast to youth and beauty." Both were social climbers, who asked famous society women to endorse their products in advertising. But most women in America were far more interested in looking like Greta Garbo than Mrs. Vanderbilt.

As the free-spending days of the Roaring Twenties crashed to an end, so did the flapper images of such stars as Joan Crawford and Clara Bow. Crawford, in particular, wanted a new look, one more appropriate for the dramatic roles she wanted.

Her request could not have come at a better time. There had been notable advances in lipstick. During the early days of World War I in Europe, America's Maurice Levy of the Scovill Manufacturing Company produced and distributed sticks of lip coloring in a protective metal casing, with levers on the sides to slide the lipstick up and down. Two common recipes at that time included crushed insects, beeswax, and olive oil, or pigmented powder mixed with butter or lard, but both turned rancid within a few hours. In 1923 James Bruce Mason Jr. patented the first swivel lipstick. There were dozens of others who had registered patents for different lipstick shapes and dispensers. By 1930 Max had not only developed his own line of hygienic lipsticks, he'd created lip gloss, to give actresses a "wet lip" look.

Joan Crawford regularly saw Max during her early years in film as a dance-happy flapper favorite. He called her "a ball of energy." Full of vitality, she was often restless in the make-up chair, but she watched patiently as Max smeared lipstick across her lips, beyond her natural lip line, for a much fuller look. Max called the new Crawford look, which became her trademark, "the smear." To the public, it was better known as "hunter's bow lips."

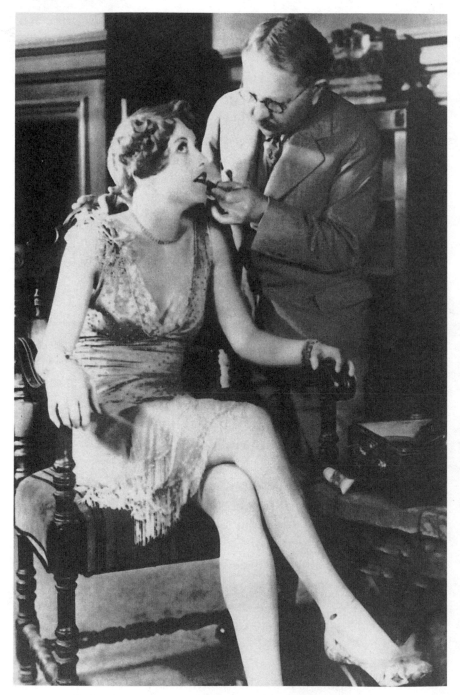

Joan Crawford in the make-up chair, ca. late 1920s.

Jean Harlow's transformation from a natural blonde to a platinum blonde for the 1930 film Hell's Angels *launched a national craze.*

To complement Crawford's lips, Max gave her dark eye make-up, which made her large eyes seem even larger, and a sculptured, wind-tossed bob she popularized. It was a harsher, more brittle look for Crawford, but it served her well in the coming years.

Soon after Jean Harlow was signed by Howard Hughes to replace Greta Nissen in the 1930 World War I aviation saga, *Hell's Angels*, she was brought to Max with instructions to "effect an alteration in her appearance, one that would make her nationally known and talked about almost overnight." The then barely known young actress was already blonde, but Max lightened her hair to a shade he termed "platinum blonde." Her new hair demanded heavy eye make-up and dark, thick lips to contrast with the stark paleness of her tresses. Jean Harlow became a Hollywood phenomenon. Her new look was widely copied by countless women who bleached their hair blonde. Young actresses followed suit. Even stars such as Bette Davis, Alice Faye, Ida Lupino, and Paulette Goddard, among others, became Harlow clones.

When Harlow died of kidney failure at the age of twenty-six in 1937, Max released this statement: "She was simply the twentieth century's most influential personality in the world of beauty. She set a style that will be copied for years to come."

Jean Harlow's magnetic appeal had made her a sex symbol. In her early films, the original blonde bombshell played flashy, trashy floozies, but she wasn't alone. As the novelty of the talkies faded and the Great Depression wore on, sex and sin (or "S & S," for short) became a major draw for moviegoers, but the industry was in serious trouble. By the spring of 1932, attendance in New York's biggest movie houses was the lowest ever recorded. Theaters were playing to fewer patrons than ever before, and the slump was spreading across the country. Along Hollywood Boulevard, as Claudette Colbert and other stars tacked up Christmas wreaths encircling their glamorous portraits on lampposts, pioneer filmmaker Cecil B. DeMille, the movies' self-appointed spokesperson, commented, "In bad times, people seek relaxation more energetically than in days of prosperity, but they shop more for their shows. You can't satisfy them with bunk. You must deliver the goods in entertainment, and if you do, good pictures have always broken records in even the worst of 'panics.'"

It took Will Hays, president of the Motion Picture Producers and Distributors of America, to clean up an industry gone wild. He developed and enforced the Production Code to protect audiences from anything they might find objectionable, such as scenes of excessive crime or brutality, revealing costumes and sex, dirty language, even cruelty to animals. Without the code's official "Purity Seal," a film could not be released.

The Production Code, which went into full effect in early 1934, didn't impact Max. The only assignment that may have raised eyebrows was body-painting a nude Sally Rand for her engagement at the 1933 World's Fair in Chicago. Despite the fan dancer's insistence on her "artistic purposes," she was arrested for giving obscene performances. The notoriety launched her career and made her famous.

Max had experimented with body painting in the mid-1920s,

Sally Rand in body paint.

when he went to New York to demonstrate a new type of stocking called the "skin sock." Rolled-down hose had become a fad along with shorter skirts, which revealed the knees of the wearer. Rather than using pieces of chiffon to hide the knees, as was the custom, Max added a painted band to the bare area above the stocking with a design — stripes, flowers, birds, leaves, anything that complemented the pattern and color of the stocking. Max's 1920s skin socks were the forerunners of the painted legs of World War II, when nylon and silk stockings were impossible to find.

Prior to the Production Code Max had worked with a number of animal actors. Pete, the dog in the popular *Our Gang* comedy shorts, was played by numerous canines over the series' twenty-two-year run, but audiences never noticed, thanks to the monocle-like black circle that ringed his right eye — make-up courtesy of Max Factor. When Tom Mix complained that his

The cast of Our Gang.

horse, Tony, had the thinnest tail of all the horses in the movies, Max came to the rescue by adding extensions, giving Tony the most luxurious ponytail in Hollywood.

The sacred white elephant seen in the Pearl White silent screen serial *The Perils of Pauline* was actually a normal pachyderm with a whitewash, which the Factors claimed was the biggest individual make-up job in history. Factor researchers had discovered that white elephants were white only in random patches, but the production staff insisted on an all-white elephant nonetheless. Max also worked his magic, turning a nanny goat into a billy goat and transforming a harmless bull snake into a king cobra by fitting it with a leather hood coated with real snake scales.

The success of the Tarzan jungle films had given Hollywood a new motto: "The higher the monkey climbs, the more he exposes his behind." Thanks to the Production Code, it wasn't only the posteriors that concerned the censors and had producers calling Max for help. There were potentially revealing full-frontal views as well.

Max designed underpants of matching fur. The chimps were measured, and fur panties were made, fitted, and delivered to the studio. On set, the chimps seemed not to mind wearing them, but once under the hot lights, they ripped them off and threw them to the ground. The pants were put back on again and again, always with the same result. Nobody knew what to do until Max hit upon a more sensible solution: use females.

It had been more than ten years since the Factors had moved to Boyle Heights. To be closer to "the store," they lived briefly in a duplex on Mansfield Avenue in Hollywood, but they needed something more suitable. Max soon found a two-story house in Beverly Hills, at 802 North Elm Drive, next door to Claudette Colbert's mother. More important, his married sons and daughters

Max and Jennie Factor, in the early 1930s.

lived nearby. A spacious home with a winding staircase, it was lavishly decorated with an eclectic mix of ornately carved and richly
painted French and Italian period furniture. As a housewarming
gift, Clara Bow presented Max and Jennie with a pet monkey,
perhaps a nod to his work on the Tarzan movies.

As Max and Jennie settled into their new home, Davis paid
his first visit to France. He had been studying foreign markets,
to establish the valuable brand internationally. "Exporting will
be our next big deal," he told his associates. He had already
appointed distributors in Canada, Mexico, Cuba, and England.

As he went through French customs inspection, the official
pulled out several jars from his luggage, and asked, "What are
these?"

"Cosmetics," Davis replied with a smile.

"Cosmetics?" the inspector repeated, looking more closely at one of the labels. He examined a jar and placed it on the counter with the others. "What is your name?" he inquired.

"Factor. Davis Factor. My father is Max Factor. We manufacture cosmetics in the United States, and I'm here to see about opening a branch of our company in Paris. We intend to sell our cosmetics in France."

According to Davis, a look of total disbelief came over the custom official's face. He glanced at the products again, and started to laugh. "Sell American cosmetics in France," he snorted. "That is preposterous. France is virtually the birthplace of cosmetics. You won't stand a chance."

Davis shrugged as he packed the jars back into his suitcase. "You may be right," he told the inspector, "but I don't think so. Women are the same the world over, and we have something every woman wants. Women in the United States want it and so will the women of France."

And they did. Davis successfully opened a branch in Paris during his stay, and the orders soon flowed in. As Helen Van Slyke reported in *Glamour* magazine, "If you have ever referred to yourself as a brownette, tried a powder brush, admired a screen star's make-up, harmonized your lipstick with your hair coloring, used a lip brush, sent for a mail-order wig or hairpiece, said 'make-up' instead of 'cosmetics,' then your life has been touched by the vital Factor known as Max. For all those things were invented or coined or perfected by Max Factor, who has come to symbolize beauty on and off the screen, in this country and a hundred and one others."

8

Opening Night

Within seven years of establishing its headquarters in Hollywood, Max Factor and Company purchased land and nearby buildings for further expansion of its manufacturing and packaging facilities. The Highland building required extensive renovations, and its salon needed complete refurbishing. The Factors had grown tired of its classic look. They wanted a more imposing showcase building in which to house their operations, something modern that was more in keeping with the times.

After exploring the possibilities, the Factors decided to stay where they were. To do that, however, the building had to be completely gutted from top to bottom, and a new edifice redesigned, inside and out. In late 1934 the family moved the store to temporary quarters, and retained S. Charles Lee, internationally renowned architect of many of the world's most beautiful theaters, to design the new structure.

Born Simeon Charles Levi in Chicago in 1899, S. Charles Lee grew up surrounded by the works of famed architects Frank Lloyd Wright, Cornelius and George Rapp, Louis Sullivan, Daniel Burnham, Irving and Allen Pond, Martin Roche, William Holabird, and the firm of Graham, Anderson, Probst & White, whose design for the Wrigley Building, completed in 1924, especially impressed him. His favorite building, however, was Sullivan's design for the Carson, Pirie, Scott and Company Building in Chicago's Loop.

Like Max, Lee was short in stature and had a fascination for the movies, having seen "flickers" in storefront nickelodeons evolve into a major entertainment. Downtown Chicago was a mecca for moviegoers and showcases, such as the Rapp brothers' glorious Chicago Theater.

After high school, the teenage Lee had worked for the architect Henry Newhouse, who specialized in theater design. He went on to study architecture at the Armour Institute of Technology. Led by his interest in the movies, Lee arrived in Los Angeles in 1922. By the time the Factors asked him to redesign the Highland building, he had already been hailed as Southern California's finest theater architect for his work on the Tower Theater, Fox Wilshire Theater, Los Angeles Theater, and the Hollywood-Western Building, among others.

Lee envisioned a modern art deco building, with detailing typical of the French Empire period. According to Frank's notes, this "striking, original combination" was enthusiastically approved. The front featured fluted pilasters extending the full four-story height of the original building and two-story addition, from a base of elegant Westfieldian green marble that surrounded the massive double-door plate glass entry and the five display windows. Directly above the main entrance, in large silver letters, it read: MAX FACTOR MAKE-UP STUDIO. Inside, wide, curved marble steps, framed by bronze railings with art deco details, led to the imposing oval-shaped salon decorated in ice blue, cerulean, and ivory. The room was carpeted in rich burgundy and lit by specially designed chandeliers of spun glass. Adjoining the salon were four spacious, air-conditioned make-up rooms with décor to showcase Max's Color Harmony principle. One room, "For Brownettes Only," was in flattering soft peach; another, "For Brunettes Only," in dusty pink; still another, "For Blondes Only," in powder blue; and the fourth, "For Redheads Only," in soft green. The name of each room was hand-lettered on its door.

Upon the redesign's completion, visitors hailed the new make-up rooms as the most modern and luxurious examples of interior design, rivaling the richly appointed dressing rooms of the stars in the motion picture studios. At the touch of a switch, one antique-mirrored wall disappeared into side panels, revealing a completely equipped make-up table with hot and cold running water and a lighting system that could be adjusted to mimic daylight, normal home lighting, even that of a ballroom or nightclub without casting shadows on the face in the make-up chair.

Behind the salon and the four make-up rooms were the cosmetic research and development laboratories, including analytical and biological labs, as well as an elaborate perfume laboratory. This complex of Factor laboratories was said to be among the finest and best-equipped in the world. On the top floors were the executive and general offices, the hair department, and manufacturing and packaging facilities. The newly added adjacent building housed a huge face powder plant, capable of producing twenty thousand pounds of powder in a single day, along with shipping and loading docks.

The Factors planned no ordinary celebration for the opening of the new building. They wanted something "super-grand," as it would mark the first time in Hollywood history that any business or building, other than a movie theater, had made its debut with a motion picture–type premiere. After months of preparation, the stage was set for Tuesday, November 26, 1935. Colorful banners were strung across Hollywood Boulevard for blocks in each direction as three thousand elaborately designed, oversized invitations (as big as a restaurant menu) were prepared for delivery, not by mail but by Western Union, signature required.

The invitation, sealed in gold cellophane and tied with a tasseled blue silk cord, read: "Your presence is cordially requested to a private party for notables of the film industry to include a preview of Max Factor's new make-up studio, Tuesday afternoon and evening, 1666 N. Highland Avenue, Hollywood, Cal. Cocktails and entertainment from four to ten." A personal letter, signed by Max, accompanied the invitation. "With pardonable pride," it read, "we invite you to attend our party and inspect our new make-up studio. The growth of our organization has naturally been made possible in no small measure by the advancement of the motion picture industry during the past quarter century. Our sincere appreciation for the splendid spirit of cooperation shown by all our friends we feel can be best expressed by our renewed promise of the highest possible standard of make-up service in the years to come. Designed with this thought foremost, our laboratories are recognized as the finest in the world. So that you may actually view the scientific creation, development and processing of make-up preparations, we have arranged to have our organization in full operation for this occasion. We shall be greatly honored by your presence."

On the morning of November 26, workers installed a large awning in front of the building, stretching from the curb to the entrance, and unrolled a wide red carpet on the sidewalk. It was still early in the day, but people began to gather on both sides of Highland Avenue. By late afternoon, the sidewalks were jammed with anxious onlookers waiting for the arrival and a glimpse of their favorite stars.

As dusk fell, police diverted traffic to side streets, allowing only invited guests through. Then the Max Factor building was suddenly illuminated with spotlights, as brilliant beams of Klieg lights crisscrossed the night sky. In its December 5, 1935, edition, *Time* magazine reported, "Great spotlights tickled the sky over Hollywood one night last week. . . . Raspberry floodlights bathed the south side of a building near Hollywood Boulevard whose fluted white front bore the architectural devices of Greece, the French Empire, the U.S. Cinema. Under the marquee passed film folk and thousands of others who had been summoned with great powder-blue and orange cellophane invitations to attend

Klieg lights fill the Hollywood sky to announce the grand opening of the new Max Factor Make-Up Studio, 1935.

the opening of the 'world's greatest cosmetics factory' — the new $600,000 studio of Max Factor."

The doors opened promptly at 4 p.m. Minutes later, stars, producers, directors, and cinematographers, longtime personal friends of the Factors, began to arrive. Chauffeured limousines drove up to the entrance, and publicists escorted guests down the

The newly redesigned façade and entrance of the
Max Factor Make-Up Studio, 1935.

red carpet to the microphones at the entrance, where they stopped for interviews. Each time a popular star showed up, flash-bulbs popped and a great roar went up from the crowd lining the street.

Once inside, guests were given a gift — an engraved silver and gold compact — then directed to a smiling Max Factor, who was waiting to welcome them. He wore a new, beautifully fitted tuxedo, and stood on a velvet-draped platform to give him some height and better positioning for the cameras. He was photographed with thirteen-year-old Judy Garland, who wore a Russian-style coat and hat as a tribute of sorts to Max's past. In another shot he was embraced by Jean Harlow and her mother, Mama Jean, and nearly disappeared in billowing clouds of fur.

Newsreel cameramen from Pathé News, Fox Movietone News, Metro News of the Day, and Paramount News stood directly opposite Max to record the event on film to later show in theaters. Hymie Fink, one of the best and most famous still photographers of the time, took hundreds of exclusive shots that evening, then sold them to newspapers and magazines around the world.

Judy Garland poses with Max at the grand opening.

Also in attendance were identical "doubles" of Mae West, Claudette Colbert, Jean Harlow, and Irene Harvey, made up by Max to look like the real stars. They were there not only to add to the excitement but to have their pictures taken for publicity shots. Jean Harlow reportedly took a liking to her starstruck double. "Call my secretary at this number," Harlow supposedly instructed her lookalike, "and she'll make arrangements for you to work on the set as my double for a few days."

Once the guests had greeted and congratulated Max, they were shown down a short hallway by beautiful starlets in evening gowns who, acting as hostesses, invited everyone to sign the huge "Scroll of Fame" — a blank parchment canvas mounted on a solid mahogany frame, positioned on a red-carpeted, three-tiered platform, and lit by colored spotlights from all sides. Claudette Colbert, Bela Lugosi, Betty Grable and her husband-to-be Jackie Coogan, Barbara Stanwyck and her husband-to-be Robert Taylor (who met for the first time at the party), Joan Crawford, Luise

*The Scroll of Fame, signed by hundreds of stars
on the evening of November 26, 1935.*

Rainer, Ann Sheridan, George Burns, Gracie Allen, Rosalind Russell, Irene Dunne, Carole Lombard, Jean Arthur, Sid Grauman, Edward G. Robinson, and hundreds of others signed the Scroll of Fame, which is known today as the largest and most complete collection of celebrity signatures of the era.

From the Scroll, guests followed a series of one-way signs to a velvet-draped elevator, manned by Factor's head make-up artist, Hal King, who took them to the top floor, where they saw everything from cosmetic chemists at work to manufacturing and packaging operations, even make-up applications. *Time* reported, "From the largest powder bin in the world, face powder was meticulously sifted through silk gauze by means of an electrical shaker appliance. Guests beheld, in glass cages, the raw materials of cosmetics. They even browsed in the Max Factor Research Library."

One of the most fascinating attractions was the Beauty Calibrator, a futuristic-looking device Max created in 1932 to reveal how a person's facial measurements differed from those of the "perfect face." Resembling a catcher's mask, or a torture device in a horror movie, its tiny thumb screws adjusted flexible metal bands that pressed gently and closely to the wearer's face; the Beauty Calibrator was reputedly capable of measuring good looks to within one-hundredth of an inch. Once the wearer's facial measurements were compared to the "perfect" measurements, corrections could be made with cosmetics to provide a "perfect" illusion. Small eyes could be made to appear larger, big eyes smaller, noses slimmed, widened, lengthened, or shortened, jawlines defined, and much more. But the Beauty Calibrator was one of the few things, if not the only thing, that Max abandoned in his ongoing quest to enhance a woman's natural beauty.

Another exhibit that fascinated the wandering guests was Max's contribution to the newest wonder in entertainment: television, which was still in its formative years of development. As early as 1932, Max and his son Frank had begun work to create make-up for the medium. They had initiated collaborative

The Beauty Calibrator revealed how a person's facial measurements differed from those of the "perfect face."

research with Don Lee's Los Angeles Experimental Television W6XAO, which resulted in a new make-up line of many different shades. A form of the recently created Panchromatic make-up for sound movies, it had been fairly successful in tests, mainly because the images projected from the Iconoscope cameras then used for television were so poor and blurred by static that the subjects were barely visible. Nevertheless, Max trademarked the term "television make-up" on June 6, 1933. (Further research was interrupted by escalating conflicts overseas, which led to World War II, but resumed shortly after the war. In March 1946 the Factors announced the first make-up created specifically for black-and-white television.)

There were bars and buffet tables on each floor. The Vendome — one of the highly successful enterprises owned by Billy Wilkerson, founder of the influential motion picture trade paper the *Hollywood Reporter* — catered the event. Wilkerson jokingly called the Vendome "the highest priced grocery store in the world," since it was a combination restaurant/store, where only the most expensive gourmet food was available to its almost exclusively motion picture celebrity clientele.

The Factors expected one thousand of the three thousand who had been invited to attend, but it appeared that everyone on the guest list was there . . . and possibly even some who weren't. The buffet dinners, which were supposed to last all evening, had disappeared within a half hour, sending the caterers running in relays for more food. Police reported a staggering number of people outside, no longer on the sidewalks but filling the street, and estimated that over ten thousand people had gone inside during the evening. It was election day in Los Angeles and all the bars were closed, but in the Max Factor building, drinks were free.

Finally, the fire department refused to let any more people in the building. Late arrivals were stopped and ushered back outside. A few stars, VIPs, and important press representatives, including Wallace X. Rawles, the bureau chief of International News Service, had to be rescued by members of the Factor staff and smuggled inside.

Meanwhile, the society orchestra of Manny Harmon played on as the evening's master of ceremonies, Leo Carrillo, one of Max's closest friends, presided over the ribbon-cutting for the opening of the new make-up rooms. Claudette Colbert handled the honors for the "Brunettes Only" room; Ginger Rogers, a redhead at the time, cut the ribbon to the room for redheads; Rochelle Hudson officially opened the room for brownettes; and Jean Harlow dedicated the room for blondes. Max posed with each of the stars, then with all four together. As Frank remembered, "His face was flushed and his eyes were bright. He was having his night and loving it!"

Max had intended to give a short speech, but when the time came, he couldn't. Seeing so many friends and hearing their hearty well-wishes had so touched him that he felt he might break down if he had to speak. "My father never could really describe the goings-on of that evening," Frank later noted, "and I really can't either. There were just too many things happening, too many people wishing us well, too much emotional strain for all of us. When we finally closed the doors, well after midnight and into the morning, we were all exhausted, but none of us had ever been happier." It was after 2 a.m. when the last guest left the building. The evening had been a long but good one, they all agreed.

Several days later Max Factor asked Columbia Studios to send a starlet to pose for a series of publicity photos, to be taken throughout the new make-up studio, laboratories, and cosmetic manufacturing areas. The next morning two girls appeared. One was an attractive brownette named Rosina Lawrence. The other was a slender, rather shy brunette called Margarita Cansino. Max personally escorted the young ladies throughout the building as photos were taken. Margarita returned frequently for make-up consultations and more publicity shots. Soon she had a new look — another hair color (red), a different hairline (Max had advised electrolysis to remove the hair on her temples and forehead), fuller lips, tweezed eyebrows, shaded cheekbones — and a new name, Rita Hayworth. She was on her way to becoming a big star.

Max Factor's solid relationship with celebrities and the film industry had Elizabeth Arden making plans to head west from New York, but when she saw Helena Rubinstein pictured with Mae West during a visit to Hollywood, she escalated her move.

Rita Cansino, the future Rita Hayworth,
poses with Max for a publicity photo, 1935.

Arden arrived in Hollywood in March 1935, eight months before
Max Factor's grand opening made international headlines. She
created a division called "Stage and Screen" and tried to woo
celebrity endorsements with lavish parties. She invested heavily
in her new project, but it quietly folded. At the same time, the
Westmore family, who had an exclusive contract to staff the
make-up departments at Paramount, Warner Bros., MGM, and
RKO, opened their own Hollywood make-up salon. But Max
Factor's domination of the field was unquestioned.

Rita Hayworth, at the height of her popularity, in 1942.

9

Crowning Glories

Max Factor was passionate about hair; it was his first love. As a child in his hometown of Lodz, Poland, he apprenticed to a wigmaker. He made wigs for the Imperial Russian Grand Opera. His ability to cut and style hair had carried him through rough times in America. Before the fledgling motion picture industry discovered his make-up, it was haircuts, switches, and wigs that kept his storefront business alive. As Frank recalled, "It took quite a long time for the new motion picture make-up to fully catch on with the studios or to supply our family with a really important source of income. More of the revenue first came from the crafting of wigs, beards, and hairpieces for the legitimate theater productions than could be gained from the early sale of cosmetic make-up materials." From the 1920s to the 1970s, all the wigs and hairpieces seen in motion pictures were made by the Max Factor hair department, with sales and rentals rivaling, often surpassing, those of the company's cosmetics.

Max began by single-handedly creating hairpieces. As his children grew older, he taught them the art of wigmaking. By the time he moved his business to Hollywood in 1928, the hair department had become a major operation. Max insisted on using pure virgin hair that had never been touched by coloring or any kind of permanent waving. He was such a fanatic about hair that he could distinguish the good from the mediocre and the bad by smell, just like a cigar aficionado can tell a good cigar.

Finding virgin hair in America was almost impossible, so he bought exclusively from Europe and Asia. Factor hair experts traveled twice a year to villages and small towns far from the cities, at the time paying $16 to $60 a pound (three or four good heads of hair comprised a pound). Some areas were so remote that the women were paid in pots, pans, and quilts, or other household goods, as money was of little value to them. Hair that was lighter in color and finer in texture was more valuable. Long, pure white hair was the most expensive, costing $60 an ounce, followed by gleaming red hair. The highest price ever paid by the Factors was to a Romanian woman in 1934 for hair that was fifty-two inches long, orange-amber in color, and finely textured. It was auctioned at a hair mart in Hamburg, Germany, and the Factors won it with a bid of $64 an ounce. It weighed twelve and a half ounces.

Native American hair, often in demand for western films, was never commercially available. The long, strong, lustrous black hair worn by movie Indians for decades came from India and China. The only animal hair suitable for wigmaking was the yak's, which was interwoven with human hair for long-shot camera scenes and used for facial hair. Yak hair was also indispensable for Santa Claus hair and beards.

The tremendous growth of the hair department in the 1920s led Max to hire Perc and Ern Westmore, sons of George Westmore, director of MGM's make-up department. For years, toupees and wigs made by Max had bases constructed of almost invisible silky human hair lace rather than thread, which made possible a more natural-looking partition. The Westmore brothers suggested using hair lace for hairlines as well. Attached to the forehead and sides with spirit gum, it virtually became part of the wearer's skin, and was undetectable when covered with make-up and powder. Called Percern — a combination of the brothers' first names — the new wigs generated enormous interest and sales.

The Westmores remained with Max until 1935, when they went on to careers of their own as head make-up artists, Perc at Warner Bros. and Ern at 20th Century-Fox. The brothers sold their patent for Percern wigs to Max for one dollar and a percentage of the rentals of all Percern wigs for a number of years. With the departure of the Westmores, the Percern name was dropped in favor of Max Factor Hairlace Wigs, a term Max had used earlier.

The vacancy opened the door for Fred Frederick, who had long wanted to work for Max. Hired by Max Firestein, vice president in charge of the department, he remained with the Factors for nearly four decades. There were only twelve people working in the wig department when Frederick arrived, but the numbers soon swelled. By 1945 he had forty-five people working with him, and by the 1960s more than a hundred.

In the old days, wigmaking was done exclusively by men, the craft having been handed down from father to son. Although times had changed, finding trained wigmakers was difficult. And the training for Max Factor wigmakers was long and expensive; apprenticeships took three years and cost the company about $2,000 per worker annually.

In making a wig, each strand of hair is tied or woven onto a wig base. It's a process called "ventilating," and workers who have mastered the technique are called "ventilators." In well-made wigs it appeared as if hair actually grew from the base. The tiny knots were invisible. At the Factor building, ventilators worked in individual cubicles supplied with bright clip-on lights. Those working with white hair, however, required extra-bright lighting to weave and tie the single strands of white hair onto the wig base of netting. A special area was set up for them on the top floor under a skylight that, with the light reflecting off the white hair, at times caused excessive eyestrain. Ventilators often wore

Ventilators at work in the wig department, where shelves of the stars' balsa-wood head molds line the back wall.

sunglasses to prevent temporary "snow blindness." Each Max Factor wig contained an average of 135,168 individual strands of hair. A full beard consisted of about 60,000 separate hairs, a Vandyke beard about 12,000, and a normal mustache about 7,000.

In the processing room, the largest stock of human hair in America was stored according to type, color, and length. There, employees called "mixers" blended strands of different-colored hair until they created the right tint. It was an exacting job: coal-black hair is seldom all black, often containing at least a few strands of red. And gray hair is actually a mixture of black or brown and white.

Max was a frugal man, possibly because of his modest European upbringing. Confronting Fred Frederick one day, he said, "Fred, you must talk to your people about picking up the hair that falls to the floor. After all, we can reuse it. Tell them to stop wasting pins, too."

Mentioning the hair was understandable, especially since white, blonde, and red hair were practically worth their weight in gold. But pins were inexpensive and thousands were used each day in the dressing and styling of the wigs and hairpieces.

Later, when Max returned, he was pleased to see very little hair on the floor. But there were pins still scattered all over. Without a word, he walked over to a table, selected the largest of three bowls, and began picking up pins, putting them in the bowl. He didn't stay long but he repeated the exercise over the next three days. The workers finally got the message, and from then on the hair department floors were pin-free.

The back walls of the wig department were lined with shelves holding the balsa-wood-carved head molds of the Hollywood stars. Measuring the precise contours of a star's head was the first step. A wig block was then molded to the exact size and shape. The blocks were conceived to save the stars time away from the movie set. Once a star was cast in a film, the studio sent sketches of the character's hairstyles. The Factor wig department took it from there, using the balsa-wood head for fittings. Once the wigs were completed, the actor or actress came in for a final fitting. Five or six wigs were usually prepared for each character's hairstyle in the film, making it possible to continue shooting the next day while the previous day's wig was washed and restyled. A female star often wore multiple hairstyles during a day's filming. By the late 1960s, the Factor wig department had over nine hundred balsa heads.

Wooden shoes were part of the equipment in the hair department. These shoes, shaped much like a human chin, were used to craft facial hair. Souvenir snips for the glued-on chin whiskers of Errol Flynn in several roles were much sought after by his fans.

Virtually every star in Hollywood wore wigs or hairpieces during their career. Even the Kewpie doll wore little sprigs of real hair styled by Max Factor. Most movie stars wore wigs for characters they played; others wore them out of necessity. Jeanette MacDonald, for instance, had very fine, thin hair. Fred Frederick remembered a time when she had lightened her hair to make it redder. "She sent me a sample to follow for color in making her a bang to go with her new hair-do," he said. "But before I got to her she had lightened her hair again. I had to make a new bang for her seven different times before I finally caught up with her experiments. She was always just one shade ahead of me."

Joan Crawford once did some experimenting on her own, too, trimming her hair with manicure scissors, then trying to even it out to the same length. "It was like shortening the four legs of a table and trying to get them all to come out even," Frederick said. "When you do that you just keep on cutting, and that's what Joan did. Finally, she gave up and asked us to cover up the carnage. We had just a day to get her into a wig before she was due to go before the camera."

Marlene Dietrich was even more demanding. She had poor hair, which was never captured on film. She insisted that real gold dust be sprinkled into her wigs to make her appear more luminous onscreen. It was her "glamour trick," and it was expensive. In the early 1930s, the cost of gold dust in powdered form was about $60 an ounce, and approximately half an ounce was required for each wig.

Wigs were returned to the Factor hair department following a day's shooting for shampooing and a reset. When Max heard of the added expense for the Dietrich wigs, he decided to save as much of the gold as possible. He knew that combing out the wigs before shampooing would salvage some of the gold dust. After shampooing more gold would be found at the bottom of the soap

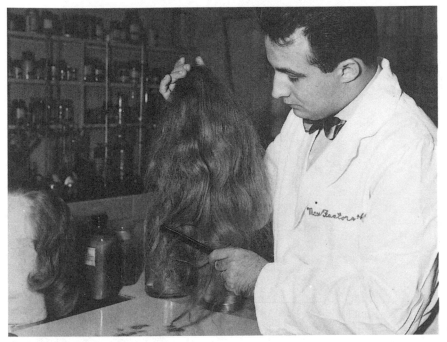

A technician combs gold dust from one of Marlene Dietrich's wigs.

solution. Of the $30 worth of gold dust added to each of Dietrich's wigs, up to $23 worth was reclaimed daily.

The popularity of historical dramas, South Sea island adventures, and westerns — among them *Mutiny on the Bounty*, *The Jungle Princess*, and *The Last of the Mohicans* — had studio orders for hair goods on the rise. Mixers and ventilators in the Factor hair department were working overtime. Then came a special request for the screen adaptation of Pearl Buck's *The Good Earth*. According to Chinese fashion, it was necessary to make it appear that the actors' hair had been shaved from their foreheads. Until now, actors had been forced to actually shave their heads for bald-headed roles, but Max made the practice unnecessary when he created a lifelike rubber "scalp." Drawn tightly over the actors' hair, it was flesh-painted and blended into the real scalp.

For MGM's lavish 1938 production of *Marie Antoinette*, the Factor wig department received its biggest order to date: 903

A bewigged Norma Shearer in the title role of Marie Antoinette.

classic wigs of pure white human hair — at an average cost of $385 per wig — for the principal players, including Norma Shearer as the title character, and 7,997 additional wigs for lesser characters.

For *The Wizard of Oz*, the hair department supplied the over-sized cat whiskers, tawny ruff, and wig that transformed Bert Lahr into the Cowardly Lion, and the strawberry blonde waves for Billie Burke's Glenda the Good Witch. Judy Garland had a series of wigs in all lengths, types of curls, and colors, from blonde to red to brunette, before finally settling on a reddish-brown piece. And twelve-year-old Elizabeth Taylor had moviegoers holding their collective breath when Mickey Rooney, blunt scissors in hand, cut her long tresses so she could ride her horse in *National Velvet*.

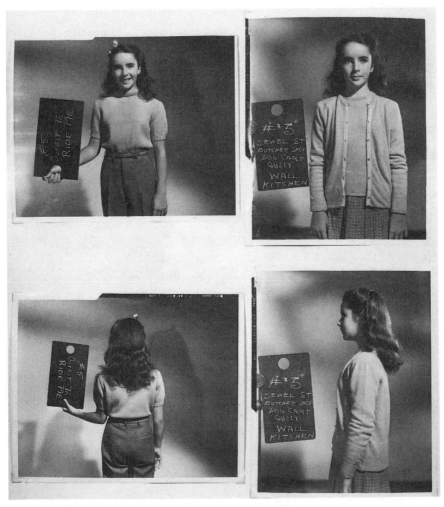

Elizabeth Taylor, wearing a Max Factor hairpiece,
in test shots for the 1944 hit National Velvet.

Actually, what he was cutting was not Elizabeth's real hair but a Max Factor hairpiece.

In 1947 the hair department received its second-biggest hair order: 4,402 wigs for the period drama *Forever Amber*, based on the scandalous best-selling novel by Kathleen Windsor. Only months later came another impressive order for another period drama. Ingrid Bergman did not want to cut her hair for her starring role in *Joan of Arc*, but the studio insisted. Fred Frederick had just completed the longest research job in the company's history — eight months and five days — to ensure the historical accuracy of the wigs he'd be assembling for the film. When Bergman arrived for her appointment with Frederick, her hair was long, down to her waist. The role of the French religious icon and war hero required

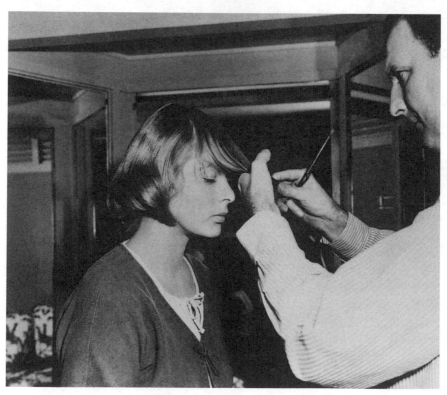

Fred Frederick of the Max Factor hair department cutting Ingrid Bergman's hair for her role in the 1948 movie Joan of Arc.

a short bob. The haircut was a traumatic experience for Bergman, but she sat quietly as Frederick clipped. Audiences loved the Bergman bob. It became the rage across America.

A good haircut or wig was not for actresses alone. Few male stars allowed themselves to be photographed, or even seen in public, without their synthetic tresses. John Wayne kept three hairpieces handy, each with the hair trimmed to a slightly different length. He'd wear the shortest one for three or four days before switching to the slightly longer one. After another few days, he'd wear the longest one, managing to create the illusion that he needed a haircut. Then he'd start all over again, making it look like he'd just visited a barber.

One day the Factors received a call from Wayne on location in Arizona. "Something's happened to my long hairpiece," he said. "Send me another one." A perfect match was on its way to him the next day. John Wayne wasn't trying to hide anything other than his balding pate. Whenever anyone asked him if his hair was real, he'd reply without hesitating, "Sure, it's real. It's just not *my* real hair."

Both Edgar Bergen and his dummy, Charlie McCarthy, wore Factor hairpieces. In fact, three exact replicas were made of Charlie's wooden head for "stand-ins," one to correctly measure and fit his custom hairpieces, one for make-up tests, and a third, which was kept at the studio, for camera setups and lighting. Charlie McCarthy was the only "star" to have sandpaper among his make-up supplies.

When one of Jack Benny's hairpieces failed to arrive at the Los Angeles Theater where he was appearing onstage, he called Fred Frederick. The delivery boy, Frederick told the comedian, had arrived at the theater early and the front door was closed. Not thinking to check the stage door, he returned to Hollywood with Benny's package. Jack Benny was unfazed, and laughed off the incident. As always, he carried a spare with him.

After World War II, the Factor hair department had its hands full with returning servicemen. According to Fred Frederick,

"Most of them came in here because they were about to go home to see their wives and sweethearts, and they wanted desperately to look just as they did when they left." Most of the servicemen's hair loss, Frederick said, came from wearing helmets, which had ground dust, dirt, and sweat into their scalps.

As noted in the August 23, 1954, issue of *Time* magazine, the Factor hairpieces were made "almost invisible by sewing each strand of hair to a piece of flesh-colored lace, sold in every style from romantic waves to college-boy crew cuts. Now men all over the U.S. wear Factor 'toups' (price: up to $150 apiece) and the company sells 70,000 a year." *Time* went on to mention that in Hollywood, nine out of every ten male stars over the age of thirty-five wore "hair additions," and listed among them Bing Crosby, Henry Fonda, Gene Kelly, Humphrey Bogart, Jimmy Stewart, George Burns, Gary Cooper, and Fred Astaire.

For those men who didn't want to be seen going in through the main entrance of the Factor building, a special door on the south side allowed entry without notice. For the thousands who were unable to come to Hollywood, Max Factor devised a self-measure chart that enabled them to order custom-made hairpieces by mail — with an unconditional guarantee of perfect fit and completion. Aside from the head measurements, all they needed to send were a hair sample for color and texture and a head shot taken before the hair loss.

During the 1960s Max Factor and Company introduced Flatter Wigs, prestyled wigs for everyday women. The new line was followed by the Wigless Wig, which reportedly did not look, feel, or "act" like a wig. Made of Elura Modacrylic Fiber, the Wigless Wig was offered in more than twenty different shades and such styles as the Mini-Fall, Classic Page, British Bob, and Elegant Cascade. Max Factor Flatter Wigs set the fashion for affordable wigs for the average woman. But by the 1970s Max Factor had serious competition from less expensive over-the-counter synthetic wigs. In 1973 new company management and ownership decided to close the Max Factor hair department. The times were changing.

10

Discovery

*I*n 1915, as Max Factor was gaining a foothold in the young film industry, working from his little store on South Central Avenue on the edge of downtown Los Angeles, Dr. Herbert Kalmus and three associates were forming a new company called the Technicolor Motion Picture Corporation. The word "Technicolor" was coined by Dr. Kalmus, a 1904 graduate of M.I.T., as a tribute to his alma mater. "It was a beautiful name," he said at the time, "a meaningful word, hard to forget, and possessing a full measure of significance for a company aiming to revolutionize the motion picture world."

Technicolor's goal was to bring color to the movies. It was not a new idea. Enterprising men, including Thomas Edison, had been fascinated with color since the earliest days of the movies, but their concepts involved either hand-tinting or toning individual frames of film, which was time-consuming, laborious, expensive, and required cumbersome equipment, such as rotating color filters. The men at the new Technicolor company were dedicated to bringing color *on film*.

Based in Boston, the Technicolor Motion Picture Corporation began operations using an abandoned railway car as its laboratory. The four partners started by making experimental films with a camera that produced a simultaneous exposure of red and green negatives, using a prism that divided the light as it entered the camera. There were many problems along the way, not only with the registration of the two colors but with the film stock and the necessary use of special projectors. Skeptics within the film community insisted that it couldn't be done, but the Technicolor technicians persisted. Experimentation continued with a series of two-color Technicolor processes, one after another, and by the 1920s the majority of studios were willing to give Technicolor a try, cautiously beginning with color sequences within features, then entire films in color. To better serve the studios, Technicolor opened new headquarters in Hollywood.

Despite the success of Douglas Fairbanks's 1926 movie *The Black Pirate*, hailed as a "glorious chromatic production," not everyone was happy. The public considered Technicolor a novelty. Some moviegoers complained that the color onscreen hurt their eyes. There were actors who rebelled at working under the hot lights necessary to capture color on film. The studios weren't thrilled with the extra cost Technicolor added to production. And it didn't help that the poor quality of films during the early years of the Great Depression was turning people away.

The Technicolor company advertised in popular magazines, using full-color ads with the tag line "Technicolor is natural color," but the brain trust at Technicolor knew it was not. Their goal was to bring full color — all the colors of the rainbow — to the silver screen, not simply the colors produced from the combination of red and green.

By 1932 Technicolor had a revolutionary new color process in the final stages of development. The company had built its first three-component camera, and one unit of its main processing plant in Hollywood was equipped to handle a moderate amount of three-color printing. Although the new process was more expensive, it more faithfully reproduced any shade or hue, indoors and out. For the first time in history, color movies were close to being realistic.

For Technicolor, however, it was like starting from scratch. Of all the studios and filmmakers, only Walt Disney was willing to give the new process a try. In late 1932 full-color Technicolor was introduced in a whimsical fantasy called *Flowers and Trees*, one of Disney's "Silly Symphonies," at Grauman's Chinese Theater in Hollywood. *Flowers and Trees* was the first Disney production to win an Oscar for Best Cartoon in 1931. This led to even greater success and another Academy Award for Disney's full-color *Three Little Pigs* the following year. Walt Disney soon signed a contract with Technicolor to produce only full-color movies.

While the studios agreed that cartoons were meant to be in color, they were still uncertain about color in feature films with live actors. The formation of Pioneer Pictures, headed by director-producer Merian C. Cooper and entrepreneur John Hay "Jock" Whitney, the cousin of Cornelius "Sonny" Vanderbilt Whitney, gave Dr. Kalmus and his associates new hope. Pioneer decided to use Technicolor for a live-action two-reeler called *La Cucaracha*, starring Steffi Duna, Paul Porcasi, and Don Alvarado. The only really big names were behind the camera: Robert Edmond Jones, the famed stage designer whose use of colored lighting revolutionized Broadway during the 1920s, was the art director, and Kenneth Macgowan was the director.

Max Factor had seen *La Cucaracha* early in its release in 1934 and Pioneer's follow-up full-length feature, *Becky Sharp*, in 1935. He made it a point to see many Technicolor releases, mostly sequences within black-and-white films. He realized something was wrong. So did Dr. Kalmus, who had a reputation for being a perfectionist. But the good doctor knew that his process was not at fault.

The make-up was to blame. Filmmakers were using Max Factor's Panchromatic make-up, created for black-and-white film, for Technicolor movies. Although thin and transparent, its greasepaint base left a slight sheen on the skin, which reflected surrounding colors. If an actor was standing near red drapes, for example, his face would have a red cast.

Many stars refused to appear in Technicolor films. Bette Davis was suspended for turning down the lead in Warner Bros.' first full-color film, *God's Country and the Woman*. Carole Lombard was another holdout, who said, "Color goes a little screwy at times, and I'm just not sure I want to make a Technicolor picture." Joan Crawford, Greta Garbo, and Norma Shearer clung to the security of their monochromatic roles.

Claudette Colbert would not even consider appearing in color films. But then, Claudette required special make-up treatment even for black-and-white movies. Despite her vast appeal, she had always felt that her face, with its wide-set eyes and high cheekbones, was difficult to photograph. And her nose was broad at its base, which required heavy shading. Even with the extra time in the make-up chair, she insisted that she be photographed only from more flattering side angles.

Max received a call from Dr. Kalmus shortly after the success of his grand opening, which was repeatedly referred to as "the party of the year." He was about to start work on a new make-up specifically for Technicolor filming, when that day, as Max stepped off the curb in front of his studio to meet a friend across the street, he did not see the approaching delivery truck and suddenly found himself on the ground. Witnesses carried him back into the salon, and a doctor was called immediately. His leg was broken, and he suffered additional incidental fractures.

While he was recuperating at home, his family and friends rallied around him as the phone calls, telegrams, and gifts mounted. During the first week alone Max received forty-three canes and walking sticks. He kept two and sent the rest to the Veterans Hospital at Sawtelle in West Los Angeles.

According to Frank Factor's records from that time, "Dad hadn't been confined to home for a week when I alone was confronted with a major problem. Technicolor had at last been perfected and was being called the greatest advance in filmmaking since sound. Although the color process had been experimented with for years, it had not, up to this very moment, been perfected to a point where it was artistically or commercially successful to the fullest degree.

"The years of laborious and costly experiment had finally paid off for the Technicolor company. Motion pictures could be photographed and screened with true color fidelity. But now a new make-up was needed for the new cinema medium, just as one had been needed some eight or nine years ago for the Panchromatic film which had come along with sound pictures."

Frank got to work, going back and forth from the Factor laboratory to the lab at the Technicolor plant, compounding make-up then testing it under full Technicolor working conditions. It became instantly apparent that no variations on the greasepaint formula, which had worked so well in black-and-white motion pictures, was ever going to meet the challenges offered by Technicolor. Once he had established this, Frank began experimenting in new directions.

"I was very thankful," noted Frank, "that by the time my father was able to walk again, using a cane, and once more able to come to our studio every day, my experiments with the new make-up for Technicolor were practically finished, and I was jubilantly happy to show him the results."

Frank had tested and retested the new make-up, but found it to be too dense. Max tested the make-up, too, and came to the same conclusion. Together, they improved the original formula until the make-up was more porous, allowing air to penetrate it and the skin to breathe. They also overcame its slight tendency toward flakiness, so that no particles were shed after the make-up was applied. Then they had the exacting task of creating tints in color harmony so delicate that they didn't destroy the transparency of the make-up.

The new make-up, which the Factors called the "T-D" series, was in a solid cake form. When applied with a damp sponge, it offered a transparent matte finish while concealing small skin blemishes and imperfections. The project was enormously complex, as Max admitted in a press release: "Previous make-ups were based on various combinations of pink, yellow, and white. Well applied, they may have looked very nice to the eye but the more critical color camera unmasks it for the glaringly unnatural thing it is. In analyzing the human complexion with a spectroscope, we found that the darker pinks, or red, are present, as well as certain proportions of yellow, white, and blue. This is true because the skin itself is essentially a translucent covering with relatively little color of its own. So our new make-up had to be made to blend with not one but a number of colors."

Frank and Max had worked for nearly two years to perfect the T-D series, even as the studios were releasing and scheduling more Technicolor productions, both for full-length features and sequences within monochromatic films. In 1936 alone, there were *Dancing Pirate*, with Frank Morgan and Steffi Duna; *The Garden of Allah*, starring Marlene Dietrich and Charles Boyer; *Ramona*, featuring Loretta Young and Don Ameche; and *Trail of the Lonesome Pine*, with Sylvia Sidney, Henry Fonda, and Fred MacMurray. Scheduled for filming were *Ebb Tide*, starring Frances Farmer and Ray Milland; *God's Country and the Woman*, with George Brent and Beverly Roberts, who replaced Bette Davis; *Wings of the Morning*, England's first feature filmed in Technicolor, starring Annabella and Henry Fonda; and *A Star Is Born*, with Fredric March and Janet Gaynor, which would include a scene with a Max Factor lookalike making up Gaynor's character for a screen test.

The first use of the new T-D make-up, renamed "Pan-Cake" for its small, flat, panlike container and cakelike form, was on the full cast of Walter Wanger's *Vogues of 1938*. The film starred Warner Baxter, Joan Bennett, who replaced Carole Lombard when she refused to appear in color, and a dozen New York models who were billed as "the most photographed girls in the world."

No sooner had production started on *Vogues* than Max Factor received a surprise visit from Natalie Kalmus, Technicolor's color consultant, who had been married to Dr. Kalmus before they divorced in 1921. As part of the divorce settlement, she became a key figure in the Technicolor company. By 1936, having established the groundwork and fundamentals for Technicolor's Color Advisory Service, she was one of the most influential — and despised — individuals in the film industry. Her presence on a set was often disruptive. Directors, as well as production and costume designers shuddered at the sight of her. Her name was far better known to moviegoers than her husband's, since it was listed as "Color Consultant" in the screen credits of every Technicolor movie until 1948.

Natalie Kalmus was a strong believer in the language of colors, and she often relied on one color to establish a mood. She insisted that backgrounds, room settings, and costumes could not clash, but had to complement one another. She conceptualized "the law of emphasis," which held that "nothing of relative unimportance in a picture shall be emphasized." Unnecessary focal points and busyness within a scene only resulted in breaking a viewer's concentration or tiring the eyes. She was, she kept reminding Max, the reigning authority on color artistry. Max listened and said nothing. But when she began lecturing him on the application of make-up for the new Technicolor movies, he left the room and did not return until she was gone.

Filming on *Vogues* began. Soon after, Pan-Cake make-up was hailed as a sensation and miracle worker. The daily rushes were proof of that, and so were the models, who were grabbing the make-up off the shelves at the studio ($2,000 worth in one week) to take home for their personal use. "It took about four times as much of the make-up necessary to finish this trial motion picture production," Frank noted, "purely because the models kept embezzling so much of it."

The only problem with Pan-Cake, the models discovered, was that they could not wear it at night; it was too dark, necessarily dark for the powerful lights used in Technicolor filming. They asked Max to make it in lighter shades, but he refused. He replied that Pan-Cake was made for the movies and should not be worn on the street. Not yet, anyway. Frank was already thinking

A Max Factor ad, featuring the models in Vogues of 1938.

ahead. Pan-Cake was not available in quantity; there was only enough product on hand for the studios, and to produce it in large quantities for general use on short notice would have been impossible. Plus they had yet to create the necessary new shades. Frank planned to wait up to a year before making Pan-Cake available to women everywhere, believing that the delay would increase demand for the product, especially once the public saw how it enhanced the beauty of the players in the "two trial movies," as he called them.

The first of these, Walter Wanger's *Vogues of 1938*, was nearing completion, and the second, *The Goldwyn Follies*, was just starting to film. Samuel Goldwyn's $2 million extravaganza featured an all-star cast headed by Adolphe Menjou, Andrea Leeds, Kenny Baker, the Ritz Brothers, Zorina, Edgar Bergen, Charlie Mc-Carthy, and the New York models seen in *Vogues*.

With his work on Pan-Cake behind him, Max made plans to travel to England for the opening of the new Max Factor salon in London, slated for early February 1937, but the long months in the lab had exhausted him. Although he did not feel strong enough for the journey, he wanted to be part of the celebration, which was shaping up to be another star-studded event, one equal to the recent reopening of the Factor building in Hollywood. Over two thousand guests were invited to the new salon at 16 Old Bond Street, where they would be welcomed by Merle Oberon. The entire affair was staged in typical Hollywood fashion, with Klieg lights, movie cameras, newsreels, newspaper reporters, lavish invitations, and innovative giveaways.

On the evening of February 5, 1937, the biggest transcontinental telephone broadcast in the history of both the American and British telephone companies was held. The first to speak with Merle Oberon in London was Ginger Rogers, who was in Stage 8 at RKO Studios in Hollywood. The call was then transferred to the Paramount lot, where Oberon talked with Frances Dee, Joel McCrea, and Ida Lupino. From there, the hookup switched to MGM, where Maureen O'Sullivan and Freddie

Bartholomew offered their congratulations. Finally, the action moved to the Factor building in Hollywood, where Gloria Swanson, Edward Arnold, Rochelle Hudson, Charles "Buddy" Rogers, Binnie Barnes, and Eric Blore took turns on the phone. Max was the last to speak with Merle Oberon and the other notables in London. He offered his best wishes to everyone at the opening and his regrets at being unable to attend. By bringing such Hollywood glamour to the event, Max Factor was credited by the British press and public as having inaugurated the biggest opening of its kind in London.

On August 19, 1937, *Vogues of 1938* premiered in New York City; five months later *The Goldwyn Follies* was playing everywhere. And just as Frank Factor had planned, Pan-Cake make-up was at last released to stores, backed by a national advertising campaign using color ads (a first for Max Factor products) and featuring endorsements by the top movie stars, which first appeared

Max Factor (center), Rochelle Hudson, Charles "Buddy" Rogers, Binnie Barnes, and Eric Blore take part in the transatlantic telephone broadcast for the opening of the Max Factor salon in London, 1937.

in *Vogue* magazine. Max Factor's Pan-Cake make-up immediately became the fastest- and largest-selling single make-up item in the history of cosmetics.

Pan-Cake became a star of the two movies, as well, singled out with raves in the reviews. Wrote one, "Make-up history in the making!" Hailed another, "Never before in color pictures have the players looked so natural and realistic. They were so lifelike, in fact, that it seemed they would step down from the screen and into the audience at any minute." For the first time, Max Factor received a screen credit, which read, "Color Harmony make-up by Max Factor." With that, Pan-Cake became the standard make-up for all Technicolor films.

Within months of Pan-Cake's astonishing success, sixty-five imitators hit the market, all called "cake make-up." Before Max, no one in cosmetics had dared use the word "cake" for a make-up product. It implied the product might be thick and heavy, rather than loose and powdery, and that was a no-no. Manufacturers had promised in advertising that make-up would not "cake on the skin." Yet it seemed every competitor jumped on the Factor bandwagon in an effort to get a piece of the Pan-Cake frenzy. But the public was not fooled. Max Factor Pan-Cake make-up was outselling them all. In fact, its sales were greater than those of the other sixty-five products combined. Max Factor trademarked the name and formula to protect the product from lookalike and soundalike competition, and took legal action against offending companies. The largest-selling competing product, Elizabeth Arden's Pat-A-Kake, was renamed Pat-A-Crème. Procter & Gamble, the giant conglomerate, approached the Factors about the possibility of manufacturing the make-up for them and allowing P&G to package it under its own label in exchange for a rich royalty. Max rejected the offer.

Once the studio heads, producers, and stars saw Max Factor's new Pan-Cake make-up, the race to film in glorious Technicolor was on. For its first full-color feature MGM teamed Jeanette MacDonald and Nelson Eddy in *Sweethearts*. Warner Bros.

reunited Errol Flynn and Olivia de Havilland in *The Adventures of Robin Hood*, a film still acclaimed as one of the finest examples of the color process. Paramount brought Dorothy Lamour to the screen in full color in *Her Jungle Love*. Fox released *Kentucky*, with Loretta Young and Richard Greene. And in the pipeline were such major films featuring Shirley Temple in *The Little Princess*, Clark Gable and Vivien Leigh in *Gone With the Wind*, Tyrone Power and Henry Fonda in *Jesse James*, Bette Davis and Errol Flynn in *The Private Lives of Elizabeth and Essex*, Judy Garland in *The Wizard of Oz*, Alice Faye and Don Ameche in *Hollywood Cavalcade*, and Claudette Colbert and Henry Fonda in *Drums Along the Mohawk*. England was not far behind the Technicolor craze, with *Four Feathers*, starring John Clements, Ralph Richardson, and June Duprez; *The Mikado*, with Kenny Baker and Martyn Green; and *The Thief of Baghdad*, starring Sabu, John Justin, June Duprez, and Conrad Veidt.

The studios' praise for Pan-Cake make-up was unanimous. MGM's Jack Dawn, RKO's Mel Berns, United Artists' Robert Stephanoff, and Universal's Jack Pierce lauded Pan-Cake not only for its beautifying effects but for its time-saving capabilities as well. The old make-up for color movies took anywhere from forty-five minutes to two hours to apply, whereas a star could be completely made up in less than fifteen minutes with Pan-Cake. The application technique, however, was entirely different and required "infinitely greater skill." During the making of *Vogues*, Joan Bennett repeatedly told Robert Stephanoff how happy she was that she didn't have to report to make-up until 8:45 a.m., rather than the usual 7 a.m., in order to be ready on the set at nine o'clock.

Pan-Cake also had the support of Hollywood's most famous cinematographers of the day, since good make-up was essential to photographic perfection. So enthusiastic were these cinematographers that many of them sent the Factors unsolicited testimonials. Harry Wild, A.S.C. (American Society of Cinematographers), who was director of photography for RKO, noted, "Pan-Cake is unquestionably the most perfect make-up I

Cases of Pan-Cake go through quality control

have ever experienced." George Folsey, A.S.C., director of photography at MGM, wrote, "With Pan-Cake, make-up ceases to be a problem as far as photography is concerned." And Harold Rosson, A.S.C., also at MGM, said, "Pan-Cake stays on longer, without repair, than any make-up I've ever seen."

For Max and Frank, these telegrams and messages from the cinematographers were especially gratifying. Early on, those same men had claimed that movies filmed in color would never be successful because of the make-up problem. They knew that color demanded a complexion finish so fine as to make it impossible to be detected. They never thought it could be done.

Max released the following statement: "The new make-up for Technicolor is the most natural preparation my laboratories have ever produced. For years I have sought to reduce artificiality in making-up stars for the cameras. With color, they appear as their true selves, just as you would see them on the street or in their homes. Natural skin tones, the beauty of their eyes, the real-life shades of their hair. Now all the stars are eager to make color pictures, knowing that the new medium will make them more beautiful than ever."

11

Moving On

The Factors were in high spirits when Max and his son Davis left for Italy in the summer of 1938. A new song, "Hooray for Hollywood," written by Richard Whiting and Johnny Mercer for the recently released movie *Hollywood Hotel*, had everyone whistling its lilting melody. The lyrics included a tribute to Max: "Hooray for Hollywood / You may be homely in your neighborhood / But if you think that you can be an actor, see Mr. Factor / He'd make a monkey look good." At the time, no one even dreamed that "Hooray for Hollywood," despite its popularity, would one day become Hollywood's anthem.

Max and Davis were traveling to Italy to investigate the possibility of investing in the newly opened Cinecitta studio outside Rome, which was looking for financial backing. The studio reportedly had Europe's most advanced production facilities with sixteen soundstages and the most modern equipment. Although Max had been advised by his doctor not to go, he was determined to make the trip. He had skipped the London opening the previous year, and he didn't want to miss this opportunity. Besides, the Cinecitta people were expecting him.

During a stopover in Paris, Max received a note demanding $200 in exchange for his life. The money was to be dropped off by Max alone at the Eiffel Tower. The gendarmes were notified and a plot was devised: a stand-in, made up to look like Max, would deliver the money.

A man of Max's size arrived at the hotel where Max and Davis were staying. He was given a mustache, gray hair, glasses, and Max's overcoat and hat, then he left for the Eiffel Tower to meet the extortionist at the appointed time. French police in plainclothes were nearby. The decoy waited and waited, but no one in the milling crowd of sightseers approached him. An hour later he returned to the hotel with the money and reported the uneventful happening.

Max was relieved but so shaken by the death threat that the hotel doctor had to be called. The doctor suggested that Davis take Max back to Los Angeles for closer examination by his personal physician. Davis booked passage on the next ocean liner back to America, one with a large, comfortable compartment. He hoped the sea air and restful atmosphere would help strengthen his father.

Once Max arrived home, he took to his bed. He died on August 30, 1938, at the age of sixty-one. At his bedside were his wife, Jennie, daughters Freda Shore and Cecilia Firestein, and sons Davis, Frank, Louis, and Sidney. They held his funeral at Groman Mortuary, with Rabbi Edgar F. Magnin officiating. Interment followed at Beth Olem mausoleum at Hillside Memorial Park in Los Angeles.

Max Factor's death headlined newspapers around the world. In Los Angeles the headlines were positioned over the masthead of the papers, a placement usually reserved for world events.

The tributes flooded in. Max Factor was hailed as "Hollywood's make-up wizard" and "the man who brought the beauty secrets of the Czar's court to America." He founded one of the greatest make-up empires the world had ever known, and was a father figure to the stars; a sweet, shy, caring, and gentle little man with big ideas who wanted only the best for his famous clientele. In an industry notorious for its big egos, he was refreshingly different. He came from humble beginnings to become a star in his own right, bigger than many of the stars of motion pictures, but through it all he was true and loyal to his associates who worked with him every day, and especially to his loving family. Frank observed, "He hadn't set out to alter the general grooming habits of women around the world, but it happened incidentally, by creating make-up materials and techniques for use in the cinema. He was one of the rarest of individuals who had lived to see literally all his dreams, plans, ambitions, and creative thoughts come to full fruition."

Only months before Max's death, Davis wrote to the company's vast network of worldwide distributors, dealers, and representatives in the Max Factor Sales Bulletin #52:

In this exciting Twentieth Century age of keen competition, when the cosmetic industry in general has become slightly befuddled with all manner of experiments in selling and merchandising, it is gratifying to know that Max Factor is the one line that has continued to operate on a selling policy which is unique, distinctive, original and successful, successful because it is fundamentally sound . . . sound because it is based on the theory of unmatched service . . . a service which was first originated for the glamorous screen stars of Hollywood . . . and later made available to the average, everyday woman in all walks of life. On this fact rests Max Factor's steady climb to the top, and to his peak success of all time in the past year.

True, there have been many imitators and, like in all things which are successful, there will be many more. But the fact still remains that there is no substitute for the genuine. Imitation is always the sincerest form of flattery, and on that premise we shall continue to look ahead and plan ahead, minding our own business, furthering our own business, forging ahead with our own business.

Now, at the peak of his company's success, Max Factor was gone. What would happen to "the store" and to the business? everyone wondered. How could it carry on without Pop?

There was no question it would go on. Max's children had worked with him in virtually every capacity. They had grown with the business and they knew it well. It had become a family enterprise, just as Max had wished, and it might never have progressed beyond a certain level had it not been for his family.

In true Hollywood fashion, Bill Hardwick — the company's publicity director, who had been hired from the studios to promote the grand opening party — suggested that the Max Factor name live on through one of the family members. But which one? Davis, the business head of the company, who had developed a sales organization, trained salespeople, and was expanding international markets and locations? Sidney, the youngest son, who also worked with the international markets and helped grow the business into Canada, Australia, Japan, and Latin America? Louis, who headed the manufacturing division and directed production? Frank, who had worked so closely in the lab with his father to create many breakthrough products, had made up countless stars, and had devised the original formula for Pan-Cake?

Or A. Bernard Shore, husband of Max's daughter Freda, who had been instructed in the art of applying make-up, was director of the salon, and the liaison with film studio executives? Perhaps Max Firestein, daughter Cecilia's husband, who had been trained in both the make-up and administrative sides of the business, worked with many of the top cinematographers, and headed the hair department?

It was rumored that the family drew straws to determine the new Max Factor, but in reality there was only one logical choice. Frank legally changed his name to Max Factor Jr.

The new Max Factor had his hands insured for $50,000. The index finger, thumb, and middle finger of his right hand were insured for $12,000 each. The remaining two fingers on his right hand and all of those on his left, being less professionally important, were covered for $2,000 apiece. He also had a curious hobby: he liked to create new perfumes. His acute sense of smell earned him the nickname "the nose." It greatly assisted him in devel-

The newly renamed Max Factor Jr.

oping custom scents and individual fragrances for every Max Factor make-up product. He had a fully equipped perfume lab in his Beverly Hills home, where he did much of his work after office hours. His days were usually filled with working with the stars. His appointment books showed that on a typical day he would see Katharine Hepburn, Fredric March, Fay Wray, Ronald

Colman, Marlene Dietrich, and Joan Crawford, who all came to the salon for either wig fittings or make-up sessions. Another entry had him scheduled to see Norma Shearer and Joan Crawford in the same afternoon. It was common knowledge that there was no love lost between the two. Crawford called Shearer the "Queen of MGM" and accused her of hogging all the plum roles because she was married to the studio's production supervisor, Irving Thalberg. As Max Jr. noted in his records, "When Norma Shearer heard Joan Crawford's laughter coming from the adjoining room she immediately stiffened and asked, 'Is that who I think it is?'

"I nodded and checked my watch. 'She's early,' I replied quietly. Norma Shearer couldn't get out of the building fast enough, but not before I made sure Crawford was behind a closed door and couldn't see her." As fate would have it, Norma Shearer and Joan Crawford faced each other a few years later in the memorable confrontation scene in MGM's hit film *The Women*.

Max Factor's death did not halt the spirit of innovation that drove his company. As it neared its thirtieth anniversary in 1939, Max Factor and Company was opening new branches in India, Mexico, and Hong Kong, and a new concept, Max Factor Hollywood Art School of Make-Up, was being planned for department stores in Buenos Aires, Santiago, Brussels, and Toronto, Vancouver, and Ottawa.

And the company continued to create custom products for film. *The Wizard of Oz* required make-up in "unusual color" pigments, particularly for the Munchkinland and Wicked Witch sequences. Margaret Hamilton's copper-green witch make-up was developed with a castor oil base that would adhere to foam rubber. Mineral oil–based make-up, initially tried, only discolored and rotted the foam. The Horse of a Different Color sequence presented a more strenuous challenge. Six horses, as identical as possible, had to be painted head to hoof in six different colors, so that on film it would seem as if one horse was magically changing colors as it pranced.

It was also in 1939 that Max Jr. returned to the lab to create a new indelible lipstick, one that was nonirritating to the lips and would not change color once applied. Indelible lipsticks had been available before, but in most cases the indelible ingredient irritated the skin and the pigments radically changed in color shortly after application.

To test the irritability and color consistency of various lipsticks as he experimented, Max Jr. asked dozens of female employees in the factory or on the assembly line to volunteer. When those initial tests proved successful, he asked for different volunteers to test the indelibility of the new product. He even requested an engaged couple working in one of the departments to come in a half hour early each morning to kiss just to see how long-lasting the lipstick really was. The young couple thought it was a great job, and they were getting paid to do it, but after a few weeks they said they'd had enough. The man was being teased by his coworkers.

Max Jr. still needed more proof of the lipstick's staying power, so he had rubber molds made of the engaged couple's lips, and the machine shop created a device with a crank on one side, along with a pressure gauge, which measured from zero to thirty pounds of pressure. It was estimated that thirty pounds was too much pressure, but ten pounds — five from "the man's lips" and five from "the woman's lips" — represented a good kiss.

With lipstick on "her" lips, and a tissue placed between the two pairs, the Kissing Machine was set in motion. The tissues were then examined to see how many lip prints registered before they started to fade. It wasn't long before the tissues were being snapped up as collectibles, not only by employees but by visitors who wanted a souvenir from the Max Factor salon.

In 1940, after months of testing various formulas and colors

The Kissing Machine, designed to test Max Factor's new indelible Tru-Color lipstick, ca. 1940.

with impressive results, Max Factor's Tru-Color lipstick was finally ready for release in six shades of red. Tru-Color was billed as "the world's first perfect lipstick . . . a lipstick that imparts a life-like red to the lips . . . that is non-drying but indelible . . . that eliminates lipstick lines . . . and that is safe for sensitive lips."

Promoted as a "once in a lifetime product," Tru-Color lipstick was often paired with Pan-Cake make-up, which was "incomparable with any products in the entire world of cosmetics." Lucille Ball was the first Hollywood actress to put Tru-Color to the test in the 1940 movie *Too Many Girls*, based on the hit Rodgers and Hart Broadway musical. She not only met Desi Arnaz during the making of the movie, she proved Tru-Color was colorfast to such a degree that it would not come off in clinches.

Make-up had come a long way during the reign of Max Factor and now his son Frank, the newly renamed Max Factor Jr. The popular look of the day had undergone numerous changes, too. Gone were the Roaring Twenties vamp with her frizzy hair and the flapper girls with their Cupid's bow lips, faces covered in greasepaint, and eyes outlined with thick mascara. Gone too was the platinum blonde hair of the 1930s, made so famous by Jean Harlow, and eyebrows that had been shaven or severely tweezed, then penciled in. Pan-Cake make-up had ushered in a new era of more natural beauty. By the end of the 1930s, shortly after the release of *Algiers*, the most popular name in the Factor make-up studio was Hedy Lamarr, an exotic, dark-haired beauty from Austria. Of all the letters received by the Factors, the majority requested make-up tips for "the Lamarr look," far outnumbering those for other such famous faces as Marlene Dietrich, Dolores del Rio, Greta Garbo, Loretta Young, Vivien Leigh, and Merle Oberon.

A new lineup of glamorous stars was waiting in the wings.

12

The Glamour Girls

There was a period when movie audiences had a hard time deciding who was prettier — the leading lady or the leading man. For over a decade, starting in the twenties, the "too pretty" faces of male stars such as Rudolph Valentino, Ramon Navarro, Billy Haines, Franchot Tone, Robert Taylor, Nelson Eddy, Gene Raymond, Tyrone Power, Don Ameche, Freddie Bartholomew, and Bobby Breen dominated the screen. But as the Great Depression wore on and the war in Europe escalated, audiences clamored for more manly leading men. In 1940 studios requested the Factors to "virilize" all the "pretty-boy" actors who were being cast as he-men in rowdy, rough roles. Although the make-up artists at the studios were responsible for much of their make-up demands, Max Jr. was asked to design the look. Here is the technique he devised:

> First, provide the subject with make-up which is at least one shade darker than that which would ordinarily be used to offer a suggestion of suntan and virile outdoor activity. The make-up may also be left with a slight surface sheen to further the impression of weather-beaten skin.
>
> For an adult, the next step is to accentuate with make-up

shadow the natural character lines which are apparent around the eyes, nose, mouth, and forehead. These lines may even be lengthened and enlarged.

For faces that are extremely youthful and callow, a slight shadow painting of bags under the eyes may be provided to offset the naturally too-innocent appearance with a worldly I've-been-around-and-seen-life effect.

The hair plays a particularly important part in providing a field for the flawing of a too-perfect appearance. For picture scenes, the subject must not show that he has been freshly barbered. His hair trim must have slight but clearly discernible touches of raggedness at the edges. In order to purposely spoil the perfect contour of a haircut, a favorite device is to cut a few wisps off the top locks so short that they will stubbornly stand erect from the otherwise smooth surface.

If eyebrows are naturally too symmetrical, they may be plucked into a slightly lopsided irregularity. This same principle may also be applied to a mouth line that is too perfect. It can be made to lose its flawless shape by creating a semblance of rugged crookedness with make-up.

A year later, on December 7, 1941, following Japan's surprise attack on Pearl Harbor, America was at war. Some of Hollywood's leading men abandoned their lucrative careers to serve in the Pacific and European battlefields, such top names as Clark Gable, Glenn Ford, Henry Fonda, William Holden, Gene Kelly, Alan Ladd, Victor Mature, Tyrone Power, Ronald Reagan, James Stewart, Robert Taylor, Kirk Douglas, Gene Autry, and Robert Stack. Many of them became even bigger stars upon their return after the war had ended. Those who remained included stars James Cagney, Spencer Tracy, Edward G. Robinson, Cary Grant, Bing Crosby, Fred Astaire, Ray Milland, Gary Cooper, John Garfield, and a few others, who were joined by those too young to enlist or be drafted or were classified by the military as physically unacceptable for service.

The news from overseas grew darker with each daily headline. Most of Europe had fallen to Nazi Germany, and the Japanese army was sweeping across Asia and the Pacific. There was rationing and shortages of many everyday products. People needed an escape from reality, if only for a few hours, which had movie attendance soaring. It was reported that motion pictures ranked high, along with food and mail from home, as vital elements to boost troop morale in the war zones. Servicemen wanted to watch movies filled with pretty girls, and they wanted to see them in vibrant full color. Madeleine Carroll had been in pictures for over a decade, in both her native England and America, but her popularity rose when she appeared in Technicolor in 1941's *Bahama Passage*. Betty Grable had appeared in twenty-eight films before she appeared in *Down Argentine Way* and *Moon Over Miami*, both lavish musicals in Technicolor. As far as audiences were concerned, they were seeing her for the first time. Noted cinematographer Ernest Haller observed, "Whenever an established star makes her first appearance in a color film the critics almost always exclaim at great length about the new personality color gives her."

The sudden attention enjoyed by Madeleine Carroll and Betty Grable, both blondes, caused Max Jr. to remark, "The blonde is coming back in favor, though in a more natural form, with ash coloring and light red favored over the falseness of the peroxide type. . . . That trend toward naturalness in screen and street make-up continues apace."

Until Technicolor, hair appeared either dark or light (or white, as popularized by Jean Harlow) onscreen. Now every tone and shade was visible, from the lightest blonde to the darkest brownette. But it was the blondes who were attracting the most attention, not only on the home front but from the GIs. Betty Grable, whose peachy complexion and shapely legs had vaulted her to top box-office stardom, was the GIs' number one "pinup girl." There were others, including newcomers Lana Turner, Veronica Lake, and Betty Hutton, along with Alice Faye, Evelyn Keyes, and Virginia Bruce, whom Max Jr. credited with being "prominently instrumental in reviving blonde popularity, first in the film capital, then all over the nation and beyond." He also noted that "this return of the blondes to favor offers a strong contrast to the Hollywood scene of even less than two years ago, when many of the most beautifully natural blondes were rushing off to dip their locks in brunette dye vats, and practically no artificial blondes were to be seen. Now there are even some stellar natural brunettes who are turning to artificial blondness just because their fancy happens to turn that way, and let the dark Lamarr tresses fall where they may." At the time, more than 60 percent of the film capital's "lovelies" were coloring their hair, mostly with rinses, which accentuated natural hair tones.

But blondes weren't alone in capturing moviegoers' attention during the war years. Rita Cansino, who had first met Max Factor as a young starlet in 1935, was now the full-fledged star Rita Hayworth. She had appeared in a number of minor roles, but it was her black-and-white photo in a 1941 issue of *Life* magazine, which showed her kneeling on a bed, dressed in a white satin and black lace nightgown, that had American servicemen overseas demanding pinup copies. Then they saw her in her first Technicolor film, *Blood and Sand*. If Rita Hayworth was beautiful in black and white, she was flawless in color. The girl with the flowing Titian tresses and sensuous manner would soon become America's "love goddess" and one of the most publicized women in the world.

There were other blondes, brunettes, and redheads, too: Maureen O'Hara, Lucille Ball, Maria Montez, Greer Garson, and Ann Sheridan. Seeing the gorgeous stars in color was probably enough incentive for the women of America to buy Pan-Cake make-up and Tru-Color lipstick, which had arrived just in time. With the war, lips had become the dominant facial feature not only in the movies but in real life. Everyone was kissing servicemen, as families, friends, and lovers bade their good-byes to the

Max Factor ad for Pan-Cake make-up, featuring Veronica Lake, who gained fame for her "peekaboo" hairstyle.

Spanish-language ad featuring Rita Hayworth, 1946.

men of the fighting forces. But the Factors weren't taking any chances. A wave of advertising appeared in magazines everywhere featuring the most popular stars of the day.

The slogan "The Make-Up For the Stars . . . and You" headlined ads in print magazines and blazed across lighted billboards. It was translated into multiple languages for use in overseas markets. One-reel motion picture shorts were also used promotionally abroad. Written, directed, and produced by William Hardwick, the Factors' public relations director in Hollywood, the shorts were narrated in as many as twelve different languages, then shipped to various countries and given free of charge by the company's branch manager or distributor to participating movie exhibitors in key cities. The tie-in gave Max Factor invaluable exposure in a medium not otherwise available. And it gave the exhibitor an entertaining, professionally produced short at no cost.

One, which was typical of the series, was entitled "The Magic of Make-Up," and showed various make-up tricks used in making motion pictures. The sequences revealed "how an actress cries, and sheds tears, in the movies," "how a woman is transformed into a man with make-up and wigs," and "how they put hair on a cowboy's chest."

For the last segment, the Factors used an unknown actor from a little theater production in Hollywood. The young man had never appeared in a motion picture; this was his big chance to get before the camera, even if it was only a one-reeler. Without any hesitation, he agreed to play the scene. The film showed him shaving his chest, then Fred Frederick, from the Max Factor hair department, stippled crêpe wool "hair" across it and secured the "hair" in place with spirit gum. When they finished shooting the tiny bit of footage, Fred Frederick commented, "We ought to put him under contract."

Bill Hardwick agreed, "Yes, he's a born actor."

Little did they know that the young actor would one day become one of the most successful stars of the silver screen: Robert Mitchum.

Pan-Cake and Tru-Color were enjoying great success, but they were not the instant solution to all make-up dilemmas. When Lena Horne became the first black performer to sign a long-term contract with a major Hollywood studio, nobody at MGM knew what to do with her. Word from the studio was that she didn't look black enough and she didn't sing the blues. Nevertheless, she was scheduled for a screen test and, rather than sending her directly to MGM make-up, a call went out to Max Jr.

In the screen test, Lena Horne was paired with Eddie "Rochester" Anderson, the gravelly-voiced comic actor on the Jack Benny show, for the nonsinging role of a maid in the upcoming film *Cairo*, starring Jeanette MacDonald and Robert Young. Lena Horne remembered, "They wanted me to match

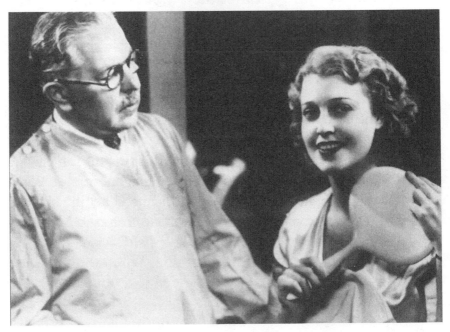

Max Factor examines Jeanette MacDonald's make-up.

Rochester's color, so they said to Mr. Factor, 'Look at this woman. Her skin's too light. Make her look colored. Colored! That's a word they used to use whenever they talked about blacks. So they kept smearing dark make-up on me." It was one of Max Factor's Egyptian shades, which pleased no one, especially Lena Horne. Ethel Waters got the part, and the early Hollywood career of this beautiful, enormously talented performer never reached its potential onscreen. Although she was rarely seen by moviegoers in the 1940s, except in specialty numbers within musicals, Lena Horne was named one of the great beauties of the decade in the Factors' "Gallery of Glamour."

Years earlier, when Max and Max Jr. developed the new make-up for Technicolor, they also created realistic-looking "blood" for the full-color process, as well as a formula for Cinecolor, a rival two-color process. During the war years, movie blood was in high demand because of the number of war pictures in production.

Wars and make-up do not seem like natural partners, but the Factors played a role in both world wars. During the early years of World War I, Max Factor supplied make-up for government motion pictures. During World War II, the Max Factor Company provided the U.S. Marine Corps with camouflage make-up in shades specifically designed to render the faces of marines as invisible as possible against backgrounds of sand, barren earth, jungle foliage, and night for the South Pacific theater. The pigment-wise chemists at Max Factor also joined the technicians at Lockheed Aircraft in perfecting a process to recover irreplaceable minerals that were wasted when spray-painting aircraft. They also collaborated on a self-sealer fluid for gas tanks on planes.

The wartime shortage of silk stockings had Max Jr. taking the art of leg make-up to a new level. According to a Factor Studios news release, "Hollywood is rather evenly divided on the timely question of make-up 'stockings.' The film capital isn't altogether sure whether it likes them or doesn't like them, or whether the vogue for the painted-on variety of hosiery will or will not endure once the war is over. But one thing is certain: screen star interest in the subject is high, and it provides a steady topic of conversation, with many different reactions being evident."

As the debate over make-up stockings raged in Hollywood and across America, the Factors were gearing up to celebrate the company's thirty-fifth anniversary with a barrage of advertising and sponsorship of a new radio show. The first of the advertisements featured the headline "Hollywood's most famous stars honor the 35th anniversary of Max Factor Hollywood," and included photographs of Judy Garland, Lana Turner, Loretta Young, Anne Shirley, Maria Montez, Janet Blair, and Ann Sothern along with their congratulatory messages. The ad ran in newspapers and magazines in every country with a Max Factor outlet.

Another ad, which ran in October 1944, was a full-color tie-in with MGM's hit movie *Thirty Seconds Over Tokyo*. Pictured were stars Phyllis Thaxter and Van Johnson, director Mervyn LeRoy, and cinematographer Hal Rosson, along with a member of the Women's Army Corps. It encouraged women to join the WAC and informed them that Pan-Cake complemented the color of the women's service uniforms. The ad reached over thirty-seven million readers through twenty-four magazines, including *Photoplay*, *Vogue*, *Harper's Bazaar*, *Mademoiselle*, *Redbook*, *Cosmopolitan*, *McCall's Glamour*, *Seventeen*, and *True Romances*.

The new radio show starred a young Frank Sinatra, who had quite a following of "bobby-soxers" as a vocalist with the Tommy Dorsey and Harry James orchestras in the late 1930s and early 1940s. He soon appeared in motion pictures, first in bit parts (usually as a band singer), then in costarring roles. By early 1945 he teamed with Gene Kelly in MGM's biggest musical of the year, *Anchors Aweigh*, and starred in his own half-hour radio show, sponsored by Max Factor.

The Frank Sinatra Show debuted on January 3, 1945, and was heard over CBS Radio nationally and on Armed Forces Radio overseas. Heard weekly on Wednesday nights, it featured such guest stars as Bing Crosby, Bob Hope, Danny Kaye, Frances Langford, Fred Allen, Shirley Booth, Rudy Vallee, Myrna Loy, and Rise Stevens, along with a full orchestra led by Sinatra's arranger-conductor Alex Stordahl.

With the end of the war in 1945, the troops returned home. Among them were the Hollywood stars who had been in the service. There was no need to "virilize" these men. They had been through hell and back, and it showed in their eyes.

The Factors reopened branches in England and France and established new ones in Ireland, Cuba, Australia, South Africa, Argentina, Italy, and the Philippines. As international business expanded, the company expressly tailored promotional programs for those markets. When asked who was the top glamour girl of the times, Max Jr. wouldn't be pinned down. He replied that his

Frank Sinatra, Max Jr., and Alex Stordahl at the Max Factor–sponsored The Frank Sinatra Show, *ca. mid-1940s.*

glamour girl to end all glamour girls had Hedy Lamarr's eyes, Loretta Young's eyebrows, Greta Garbo's nose, Maureen O'Hara's mouth, Joan Crawford's cheekbones, Irene Dunne's chin, Judy Garland's ears, Susan Hayward's neck and shoulders, Lana Turner's torso, Linda Darnell's hair, Cyd Charisse's arms, Katharine Hepburn's hands, Betty Grable's legs, Myrna Loy's freckles, Lauren Bacall's voice, and Rita Hayworth's genius for wearing clothes.

By 1947 advances in lighting and photographic effects required the creation of a new make-up. Max Jr. spent twenty-six months to develop Pan-Stik, a cream make-up packaged in stick form. He first worked with the Goldwyn Girls, the showgirls who appeared in Goldwyn musicals, then persuaded friends to try it. "Marguerite Chapman tested it for me in one of its earliest forms," he noted. "A little later Jane Greer showed me its working in a more perfected development. For olive complexions, Ava Gardner was my model. When it was nearly perfected Sylvia Sidney demonstrated its advanced workings for me. Then, by the time the new make-up was ready to go, Lana Turner, Barbara Stanwyck, Judy Garland, and Rosalind Russell had to try it out. Where else but Hollywood, and in what other business but a make-up studio for the film industry, could anyone find such famously beautiful and glamorous women to act as guinea pigs for a new product?"

To use Pan-Stik, you only had to remove the cap and turn the revolving base until the make-up projected slightly from its case, much like lipstick. You then dabbed it on your forehead, nose, cheeks, and chin. Once it was blended with the fingertips over the entire face, you powdered lightly. Non-oily and non-greasy, Pan-Stik was called "fool-proof," "amateur-proof," and "streak-proof." It could be applied completely in less than twenty seconds. "Its applications are exceptionally long-lasting," observed Max Jr., "and do not lose their freshness of appearance as the hours go by. It does not bring a tight, restricted feeling to the face but, rather, a cool and refreshing sensation to the skin. And it can easily be retouched without having to revoke the make-up." Pan-Stik was extremely popular with male actors. With Pan-Stik they were in and out of the make-up chairs in less than twenty seconds, and they seldom required touch-ups.

Created for motion pictures, Pan-Stik was trademarked in July 1948. Like Pan-Cake, it was an overnight sensation among glamour-conscious women, but not before it was first seen on Greer Garson and Janet Leigh in MGM's 1949 Technicolor romantic drama set in Victorian times, *That Forsyte Woman*. When it came to beauty, as Hollywood went, so did mainstream America.

13

Changing Times

Following the success of Pan-Stik cream make-up, in 1950 the Factors introduced its World of Beauty line. Described as "an extensive and completely new array of Hollywood skincare products," it included cleansing cream, night cream, lotion, talc, and facial soap. Available in over one hundred countries, the World of Beauty line was appropriately named. The company now employed nearly ten thousand people worldwide.

Beginning in June 1951, the Factors expanded their market by releasing the first line of grooming essentials for men, Signature by Max Factor Hollywood, said to be used by Hollywood's most famous actors. The new men's line consisted of shampoo, aftershave lotion, deodorant cologne, mousse, and shaving foam.

Max Jr. then turned his attention to make-up for television. Earlier, in 1933, he had worked with his father on experimental tests, and again on his own in 1946, to introduce the first make-up for black-and-white commercial television. Now, with continuing improvements to the medium, NBC's Color Research Department asked him to create a complete new range of special shades for color TV. Images on black-and-white television stock projected as a negative, so the make-up looked hideous on the actors, but once transmitted and reversed, appeared normal on

Make-up for black-and-white television.

TV screens. But the make-up for black-and-white TV wouldn't work for color TV, nor would the make-up for color movies. Off camera, the existing shades were pleasing to the human eye but appeared harsh, unflattering, and unnatural before the super-sensitive color television cameras.

After seven months of experimentation and testing, Max Jr. finally delivered. Television networks recommended that their stations and affiliates exclusively use Max Factor's Color TV Make-Up as the standard for all color TV programming. In 1955 Ida Lupino, on behalf of the Academy of Television Arts and Sciences, presented Max Factor Jr. with the academy's Distinguished Service Medallion for his "invaluable services to the television industry in the field of make-up for both black-and-white and color TV."

The experimentation for color TV make-up resulted in two innovative products. In 1954 Max Factor presented Erace to the women of America, and in doing so revealed a unique beauty secret used by the stars of motion pictures and television. Erace was the original cover-up or concealer applied underneath make-up to hide imperfections, lines, shadows, blemishes, and blotches from the merciless eye of the camera.

The other new product was Hi-Fi Fluid Make-Up, available in exclusive High-Fidelity colors. According to the company's press release at the time, "'Hi-Fi' does for color what high-fidelity does for sound. It makes every skin tone come vibrantly alive and faithfully reproduces gradations of natural complexion and skin color as no other make-up has ever done before. The formula contains a softening ingredient which leaves the skin soft and dewy, but never greasy."

The post-war slump in movie attendance caused the Factors to rethink their use of film star endorsements in company advertising. In mid-1952 they launched the first national Max Factor Girl contest, offering $5,000 worth of prizes along with the title. Sharon Lee Curtis from Northwestern University in Evanston, Illinois, was selected (among entries from 352 colleges and universities) as the coed who most beautifully captured the "fresh, young, natural American look." The national media covered Sharon Lee Curtis's tour of Max Factor's U.S. outlets, but she did not appear as the Max Factor Girl in company advertising. Instead, the "Fresh, Young, Natural Look" became a promotional campaign for Pan-Cake make-up and Tru-Color lipstick.

There were other reasons for the Factors' search for new faces to promote their products. The Golden Age of Hollywood was coming to an end, and the studios were cutting costs by releasing many of their top actors and actresses from their contracts, turning even the biggest stars into independent properties. As the studios trimmed their rosters of performers, shrewd business managers descended upon the free agents, aware of the gold mine advertisers could and would offer. Gone were the days of signing a major personality to a long-term endorsement contract for only one dollar.

Among the last to endorse Max Factor products were Elizabeth Taylor, Esther Williams, Donna Reed, Janet Leigh, and the very last, Debbie Reynolds. Of all the stars, Lucille Ball had the longest association with Max Factor and Company. She had signed her first promotional agreement with Max in 1935, and throughout her long career in movies and television had relied on Max Factor make-up both in her personal and professional lives. Her long-running TV show *I Love Lucy* included the credit line "Make-up by Max Factor." She insisted on the personal services of the salon's make-up director, Hal King.

In 1955, shortly after the release of Crème Puff, a new all-in-one make-up, Max Factor published an illustrated brochure entitled "You at Your Loveliest," which included the latest beauty tips along with information on other products, such as Pan-Cake, Hi-Fi, Pan-Stik, Erace, Crème Puff, and the Color Harmony chart. It also introduced Electrique, the company's first fragrance. It was a sensational success. Three years later, Max Factor launched its second fragrance, Primitif.

Max Factor had been a client of Sales Builders, Inc., the sales and distribution company, since the late 1920s. In 1956 the Factors announced the acquisition of Sales Builders. Within a year, a complete reorganization of Max Factor's U.S. marketing, sales, advertising, and merchandising division was completed. Alfred Firestein, a vice president and member of the board of directors, as well as Max Factor's grandson and son of executive vice president Max Firestein, was appointed director of the newly reorganized U.S. marketing division, which had absorbed Sales Builders. The merger and reorganization resulted in Max Factor's cosponsorship of the 1957 Miss Universe Beauty Pageant. Gladys Zender of Peru was crowned the new Miss Universe and spent

Max Jr. welcomes the 1957 Miss Universe pageant winner, Gladys Zender of Peru, and runners-up to the salon.

much of her reign as the Max Factor Ambassadress of Beauty, touring Latin American countries.

The company then embarked on a multimillion-dollar construction spree, under the direction of Davis Factor. As personnel began moving into a new $1 million building that housed the general offices and research division, only one block east of the main building on Highland Avenue, a 250,000-square-foot, $3 million plant that included warehousing facilities was rising south of Los Angeles in Hawthorne, California. The Factors also announced a $1 million expansion and modernizing program for six of the company's plants and warehouses in Hollywood.

With the acquisition of Parfumes Corday, Inc., the French creators of perfumes Toujours Moi, Fame, Trapez, and Jet, Max Factor established a stronger presence in the fragrance business. In 1958 an unexpected economic recession caused a downturn in sales and profits, but it took only six months for the company to catch up to its original forecasts.

The rebound couldn't have come at a better time. On January 2, 1959, Max Factor and Company began a yearlong celebration to mark the fiftieth anniversary of its founding, beginning with a continuous flow of publicity and news releases about the company and its products, all keyed to its golden anniversary. One of the highlights was the anniversary party, held in the salon of the Max Factor building and attended by the biggest Hollywood movie stars. The milestone event featured a three-tiered cake and celebrity lookalikes in make-up and costumes from the past five decades of film.

As the Factors entered the new decade, Class A stock of Max Factor and Company was listed for trading on the New York Stock Exchange for the first time. And new members of the third generation of Factors were added to the executive staff: Barbara and Davis Jr., children of board chairman Davis Factor; and Donald, son of president Max Factor Jr. The sons of Max Firestein, Alfred and Chester, had already become vital to the company,

Max Factor's star on the Hollywood Walk of Fame, located at 6922 Hollywood Boulevard, was dedicated on February 9, 1959.

Alfred as director of U.S. marketing and Chester as merchandising director.

By the mid-1960s, mergers were taking place all across America. Large companies turned into giant conglomerates by swallowing smaller firms. Max Factor employed professional acquisition searchers, both in the United States and Europe, to scout for potential acquisitions that would benefit the company. But Max Factor was also a desirable prize for other corporations, namely American Cyanamid. An agreement in principle to merge was reached, but the Factor hierarchy decided against it at the last moment. Then, toward the end of the 1960s and the beginning of the 1970s, a series of changes shook the executive ranks. Sidney, the youngest of Max Factor's four sons, a board member and senior vice president of the international division, resigned to work full-time for his personal enterprises. Barbara, Davis's daughter, left to become a housewife. Donald, Max Jr.'s son, decided to pursue his ambition of becoming a film producer. And Davis Jr. resigned to go into business for himself.

Alfred and Chester Firestein, as the sole remaining members of the third generation, were destined to head the company. Both had outstanding educational backgrounds and many years of experience in top executive positions. Both were enthusiastically supported by the senior family members of the executive committee. In January 1968 the board of directors elected Alfred Firestein, forty-three, president and chief executive officer of Max Factor and Company. Chester Firestein, thirty-seven, was named executive vice president and member of the executive committee. Davis Factor remained board chairman; Max Factor Jr., former president, became vice chairman of the board; and Max Firestein, former vice chairman of the board, became chairman of the executive committee.

In acknowledging the responsibilities of his new position, Alfred Firestein paid tribute to members of the second generation of the family for their aggressive leadership throughout the decades since Max Factor's death. Soon after his election to the presidency, Alfred met with David J. Mahoney, chairman of the board of Norton Simon, Inc., a conglomerate that also owned Hunt Foods and McCall's Publishing. The two attended a seminar sponsored by Felix Juda, then one of the nation's most noted stockbrokers. Juda suggested Norton Simon make a bid for Max Factor.

Merger negotiations began in the latter part of 1972. A special meeting of the shareholders of both companies was called for February 13, 1973, to vote on the agreement of a merger. Approval was overwhelming and the transaction was completed the next day, with Max Factor stock selling at a high of $42. The merger made Norton Simon, Inc. larger than fellow conglomerates Bristol-Myers, General Foods, Johnson & Johnson, B.F. Goodrich, PepsiCo, Nabisco, and CBS, with yearly earnings surpassing $1.1 billion.

But the news that followed was devastating. On March 27, 1973, only weeks after the merger, Alfred Firestein died suddenly at the age of forty-eight. Eight months later, in November 1973, David Mahoney appointed Chester Firestein president of Max Factor and Company. Under Chester's leadership, the company attained new highs in both sales and earnings. He expanded overseas markets and launched numerous new products, including the Halston designer fragrances, the UltraLucent Waterproof line (designed "to stay on perfect under all conditions — even an underwater swim"), and a series of Musk for Men fragrances.

After nearly twenty years Max Factor and Company began using famous faces in its advertising once again, only this time they belonged to professional models, not movie stars. The first was Cristina Ferrare, who appeared in more commercials and print ads than any other model at the time. Other young Hollywood hopefuls and top models who became the face of Max Factor were Cheryl Ladd, Farrah Fawcett, Bo Derek, Cheryl Tiegs, Shari Belafonte, Jane Seymour, and Jaclyn Smith.

Despite reports that overseas markets had expanded to more than 200,000 accounts in 144 countries, led by Japan and the United Kingdom, the news from the executive committee of Max Factor and Company was not positive. In 1976, after only three years as president, Chester Firestein resigned to devote more time to his personal business activities. Samuel Kalish, Revlon's high-profile, marketing-oriented leader, joined the Factor organization as president and CEO. Kalish accepted the position, he admitted, because of the challenge it presented. But over the next few years, Max Factor and Company had two other presidents, both brought in from the outside. The family was no longer involved in the company's day-to-day operations, and another merger was in the works.

In 1983, just as operations were beginning to run smoothly again under the leadership of Linda Wachner, Norton Simon, Inc. was taken over by Esmark. A year later, Esmark merged with Beatrice Companies, which made Max Factor an extension of its

International Playtex division. With the acquisition, company headquarters were moved to Stamford, Connecticut. The public knew little about what was taking place behind the doors of the Max Factor building in Hollywood, with its spacious salon, make-up rooms, and merchandising counters — until it closed. A smaller retail store with a beauty shop was opened in the one-story building next door, once occupied by part of the hair department, but it wasn't as spacious or nearly as elegant. No one knew what would happen next.

14

The Legacy

With the relocation of Max Factor and Company to the East Coast, director of beauty Robert Salvatore and his small staff tried not to dwell on the probable closure of the recently created retail store and beauty shop, the only remaining reminder of the once bustling Max Factor building. Word was out about the move, so it was only natural that most people who wandered into the new retail space asked about the future of the building.

While the hot topic of the day in Hollywood in early 1984 was the Max Factor building, Olympic fever gripped Los Angeles. The summer Olympics were coming to the city, and the race was on to complete preparations in time. Various sporting events were going to be held from one end of the city to the other, and there were concerns about traffic and road closures. Accommodations were needed for all the athletes and spectators who would be arriving from all corners of the world.

It came as a surprise to Robert Salvatore when headquarters asked him to organize a small exhibit of Max Factor memorabilia that would be open to the public free of charge during the weeks of the Olympic Games. "That's how the museum began," he recalled, "so we started painting and putting together a temporary little exhibit." Salvatore was perfect for the assignment. He had been with the company since the early 1960s, when he was brought in from the New York salon to replace Hal King, who had left to work with Lucille Ball. Salvatore had known the Factors personally. He could discuss any aspect of the company's history, and Max had long been his inspiration.

To make the experience more authentic for visitors, Salvatore knew the exhibit had to be housed in the spacious salon of the Factor building. The visiting public would walk through the same double doors and up the same marble steps into the salon as the stars had done for decades. He hired an assistant, Randy Koss, to work with him, and three attractive, congenial women: Fran Tygell, whose husband, David, had been an accountant for the Factors, Jeanne Veloz, and Betty Jennings.

Working with Factor family members, Salvatore knew he could locate enough historic items to make a fascinating exhibit. He gathered Max's earliest powder-grinding machine, his original desk, the Kissing Machine, the Beauty Calibrator, and make-up in original packaging dating back to pre–World War I days, including collapsible tubes of original greasepaint for the movies. There were contracts signed by the stars of the '20s, '30s, '40s, and '50s, photographs of the stars autographed to Max Factor, and thousands of other photos showing Max in the lab, on movie sets, working with the stars in the make-up rooms, and party photos taken at the building's grand opening in 1935. The celebrity-signed Scroll of Fame was also available. And the display cases and mirrored shelves were still intact.

While many of the wigs had been sold to collectors following the closure of the building, dozens still remained, including those once worn by John Wayne, Marlene Dietrich, Fred Astaire, George Burns, Lucille Ball, Frank Sinatra, Billie Burke, and Rosalind Russell. Salvatore also located a long-flowing wig created for Dorothy Lamour's sarong-wearing island girl in her South Sea adventures, the wig blocks of Elizabeth Taylor, Barbra Streisand, Debbie Reynolds, and Charlton Heston, as well as the head block

Max in his basement lab in the South Hill Street store, 1922.

and wig for Boris Karloff in his role as Frankenstein's monster in the 1931 film.

The Max Factor Beauty Museum opened in June 1984, in time to lure visitors attending the summer Olympics, and it soon became a major Hollywood attraction. "Young people loved it because they missed all the glamour during the Golden Age," remembered Fran Tygell, "and old-timers loved it because they grew up during that era and could identify with all the big stars and the movies. But we were surprised to discover how many people thought Max Factor was just a brand name, not a real person."

The popularity of the museum during the summer of 1984 brought positive news from headquarters. "We were allowed to keep the doors open," Salvatore said. "Then every year we were given more money to restore another room, then another, and another until we basically filled the entire main floor."

Bette Davis poses with select Max Factor products, ca. mid-1930s.

Max with Jean Harlow, 1931.

One very warm day in 1988, Arnold Schwarzenegger, blinded by the sun, walked through the museum door. "What is this place?" he asked.

"It's the Max Factor Beauty Museum," Fran replied. "I'd be glad to give you a tour."

Schwarzenegger explained that he was taking a break from filming *Twins*. They were shooting around the corner on Hollywood Boulevard, and he was looking for a place to cool off.

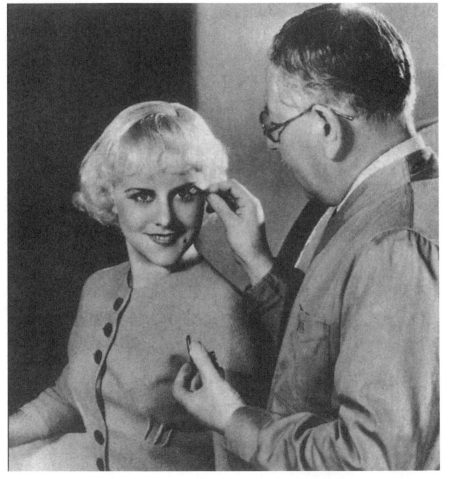

Max working on Paulette Goddard, ca. mid-1930s.

A few minutes later, Danny DeVito appeared. "Ya got a toilet?" he asked.

"I have a private bathroom," Fran replied. "You can use it, but you'll have to put the seat down when you're done."

"Oh, honey," he laughed. "I always do. There are three women in my family."

Two years later, in 1990, Jack Nicholson, Meg Tilly, and a crew filmed in the museum for two days. They were working on *The Two Jakes*, the sequel to *Chinatown*, set in 1948 Los Angeles.

Cars from the 1940s were parked outside and all the cast members were dressed in vintage '40s clothes. Following the filming, Nicholson and Paramount Studios helped restore the main salon by replicating much of the interior columns, urns, and furniture that had been lost or damaged over the years, recreating the original 1935 décor. Then they had the room filled with flowers.

Meanwhile, developments on the East Coast would affect Max Factor and Company. In 1986 Kohlberg, Kravis, Roberts & Company acquired Beatrice Companies. An adjunct to the negotiations involved International Playtex, of which Max Factor was a subsidiary. The Playtex division and its subsidiaries were sold to Joel Smilow, an Esmark/Beatrice executive. Smilow retained Playtex but sold Max Factor to Revlon's Ron Perelman. A year later, Perelman appointed Allan Kurtzman, Neutrogena's former president of consumer products, as president of Max Factor worldwide, with the stipulation that the company return to its former headquarters in Hollywood.

The Wall of Stars in the Max Factor Beauty Museum, ca. mid-1980s.

Kurtzman was no stranger to the Factor organization. He had worked for the company in 1960, when Alfred Firestein appointed him corporate vice president and director of U.S. marketing. Then came the merger with Norton Simon and Kurtzman was out of a job. Now he was back in Hollywood, settled into his office in the Max Factor building, joined by a handful of employees who had managed to survive all the moves, mergers, and takeovers. There were new faces, too, filling the upstairs offices, an energetic workforce of top talent personally selected by Kurtzman. It didn't last long.

In 1991 Max Factor was taken over by Procter & Gamble, and, once again, the company was headed east, this time to Cincinnati. The museum remained open, but its future seemed shaky. Salvatore and his staff were certain the museum's days were numbered. After all, Procter & Gamble was not in the museum business, and word was the building would soon be on the market. Despite the uncertainty, Salvatore continued with the museum's restoration and expansion. The four make-up rooms were repainted in their original pastel colors and meticulously preserved in every detail, complete with the original make-up chairs, settees, lights, and multi-angled mirrors. Down the hall visitors could sit in a small theater and watch short videos about Max Factor, while "Hooray for Hollywood" played in the background.

In May 1992 talk of the end swirled once again. Rumor had it that Procter & Gamble would close the Max Factor building in thirty days and donate all the memorabilia to a Hollywood museum that had yet to be built and was far from financed. There was an outcry from Hollywood activists, preservationists, and tour bus companies. In the short time it had been open, the museum had become a Hollywood institution, attracting an estimated ten thousand people a year, all without any advertising.

"Save the Max" advocates demonstrated outside the building on Highland Avenue. A "Fax to Save Max" onslaught was organized. Boisterous bands of celebrity lookalikes and protestors wearing "Rally to the Max" T-shirts set up a seventy-seven-day picket line. "It's a shame that all this history will be lost," said Salvatore at the time. "Hollywood has to save its history. It's all going. The tourists come to Hollywood Boulevard and they see Grauman's Chinese Theater, and that's about all that's left. Disney has restored the El Capitan, which was brilliant, and the Max Factor Museum is right here. To close something that exists and is in perfect condition makes no sense."

After months of Hollywood-style community protests, Elvis, Marilyn Monroe, and Frankenstein impersonators took to the streets again in December when a Malibu-based development firm announced it would buy the Factor building and turn it into a warehouse or manufacturing plant. Meanwhile, recreations of the façade of the building were going up in Disney World (Orlando, Paris, Tokyo), Disneyland (Anaheim), the MGM theme park (Orlando), and the MGM Grand Hotel (Las Vegas).

The uncertainty and stress began to take its toll on Salvatore. "He'd miss days of work, and he was losing weight," recalled Fran Tygell. "Then we learned he wouldn't be coming back. The only good news then was the hiring of Noreen Hinds, as supervisor, to take Robert's place. That gave us hope we'd be staying open a little longer, at least. But we all missed Robert dearly. The museum was his baby. He all but made it happen." Robert Salvatore passed away shortly before the museum was finally closed in June 1996.

The Max Factor building was sold toward the end of 1996 to Donelle Dadigan, a Beverly Hills real estate developer and passionate Hollywood memorabilia collector. The goddaughter of famed pianist/conductor José Iturbi, who had appeared in a number of Hollywood films in the '40s, Dadigan spent more than eight million dollars over the next eight years to restore the building to the original 1934 plans of architect Charles S. Lee. She hired building design craftsmen to return the exterior and interior of the building to its original art deco grandeur. She imported rare marble from Europe for the façade, as Lee had done; restored the elegant four-story fluted pilasters, duplicating the sparkle with crushed light bulbs, as inspired by Max Factor; reconstructed the elegantly curved display windows with their magnificent ornamental trimmings; and installed decorative lamps flanking the entryway.

The main foyer and grand salon were gutted and recreated according to the specifications of the 1934 plans that called for the gracious, curved entryway steps, white marble floors, 1930s color scheme of plum and lavender, and marbleized pilasters accented by twenty-four-karat gold and silver detailing. The original Max Factor display cases and landmark Color Harmony make-up rooms were also replicated.

The top floors, where the executive and general offices, labs, and manufacturing facilities once were, now housed photo galleries and spacious exhibit areas, for both memorabilia Dadigan received from the film community and her own priceless collection of movie artifacts. The basement, the long ago site of a bowling alley, was redone to hold the entire prison cellblock where Hannibal Lecter was confined in *The Silence of the Lambs* and *Red Dragon.*

Donelle Dadigan's Hollywood History Museum officially opened on July 24, 2003, with many Hollywood notables in attendance, including Hollywood's honorary mayor, Johnny Grant. Today, there are five thousand displays in the permanent collection, highlighted by costumes and wardrobes worn by Elvis Presley, Rudolph Valentino, Mae West, Lucille Ball, Bette Davis, Joan Crawford, Elizabeth Taylor, Shirley MacLaine, Nicole Kidman, Leonardo DiCaprio, and scores of other stars; Cary Grant's Rolls-Royce; Sylvester Stallone's *Rocky* gloves; set pieces and props from *A Star Is Born, Let's Make Love, Cleopatra, Flash Gordon, Men in Black, George of the Jungle, Titanic, There's Something About Mary, Gladiator, Moulin Rouge, Planet of the Apes,* and many, many more films. Special exhibits have included "Barbra Streisand: The Legacy Collection," "Bob Hope: Thanks for the Memories," and "Marilyn Monroe: The Ultimate Hollywood Icon."

The ultimate tribute, however, is the main floor, devoted entirely to Max Factor. Visitors entering the Hollywood History Museum will feel like they are stepping into Max Factor's legendary Make-Up Studio, the Hollywood of the Golden Age. On display are many of Max Factor's original cosmetic creations and innovations, first seen in the Max Factor Museum, and the make-up rooms where the most beautiful stars were made even more beautiful by the master himself. Max Factor's history has not been lost.

Across town in Culver City, Davis and Dean Factor were following in the footsteps of their famous great-grandfather. They own and operate Smashbox Studios and Smashbox Cosmetics, founded in 1991 and 1999, respectively. Smashbox Studios is a state-of-the-art, full-service photo and film studio that has hosted top models, fashion photographers, wardrobe stylists, hairstylists, make-up artists, art directors, and even L.A. Fashion Week. Davis said, "We are in the business of making women look glamorous. That's very personal to me." His great-grandfather would be proud.

In 2005 Procter & Gamble chose model, actress, and dancer Carmen Electra to be the face and spokesperson for Max Factor, and launched a print, television, and online advertising campaign for the new line.

The year 2009 marks the hundredth anniversary of the company Max Factor founded. His products are still on the lips and faces of women everywhere. The young immigrant escaped to America in 1904 to become the father of modern make-up. A true innovator and pioneer, Max made it not only acceptable but desirable for women to wear make-up, in the process creating a cosmetics empire that launched what is now the multibillion-dollar beauty industry. He didn't invent glamour, but he brought it within reach of the everyday woman. In doing so, Max Factor truly changed the faces of the world.

A Max Factor ad featuring Carmen Electra.

Afterword

Robert Salvatore had wanted to write a book about Max Factor for as long as he'd worked for the company. But he knew that probably wasn't going to happen. For nearly forty years he had seen writers being turned away almost daily because the ultracautious family members had no interest in anyone digging up the past. They had good reason to feel the Max Factor story might be sensationalized. The writers all wanted to know about Max's younger half brother, John Jacob Factor, the notorious con man and swindler better known as "Jake the Barber."

Jake the Barber was the last person on Robert Salvatore's mind when he was put in charge of the Max Factor Beauty Museum. The family had sold the business, and the company was headquartered back east. As creator of the museum he had total access to the Max Factor archives, which were filled with rare papers, unfinished memoirs, memos, journals, documents, photos, and scrapbooks of clippings and early newspaper articles. He also had access to the collection of priceless memorabilia that had been left behind. The more he discovered the more determined he became to do a book.

Robert eventually went to the family and told them of his interest, quickly adding that he had no intent to trash their father. "I want the world to know this sweet, talented man existed," he confessed, "that he created make-up for the movies, and had terrible tragedy in his life but never let it beat him down." He told them of the stories he'd discovered going through the archives and of information he'd uncovered with the help of a specialist in family research, especially about Max's early years and coming to America, when his children were too young to remember. He told them of the addresses and documents he had obtained for their years in St. Louis, before they came to California. He also mentioned the information that he'd found at the Mormon Temple Family History Library.

The Factors looked at one another, Robert reported, amazed at what they were hearing. Finally, he heard the words he had longed to hear: "If you write it, we'll allow it."

Robert wasn't a writer, so he quickly found someone to work with, but after many months the partnership fell apart. By the time he spoke with Paul Kaufman, an award-winning producer-director of documentary films, feature films, and television programs, who was filming a video about the Max Factor Museum, Robert was no longer working there.

I had met Paul Kaufman earlier when he was working on a TV project based on one of my books. He called to tell me about Robert and his search for a writer. Robert was going to be in town only a week or so longer before moving back to the East Coast to be with his family. He had already moved out of his apartment and was temporarily staying with Randy Koss in his Craftsman-style bungalow just off Sunset Boulevard. When Paul and I arrived several days later, Robert was sitting at a long plank table in the kitchen. He looked so frail I thought we would stay only a short time. We were there most of the day.

Once Robert started talking about Max Factor we could feel his energy. His voice was strong and he talked nonstop. I was glad I'd brought a tape recorder with me.

He had photos from the Factor archives, ranging from Max's days in Russia through the glory years in Hollywood. There were important stories and milestone events that had to be told, he said, listing them, along with his favorite memories of the Factors. When it was time for us to go, Robert pointed to a pile of boxes against the kitchen wall. "Take them," he said. "Everything I've told you, and a lot more, is documented. It's all there, Max's life and the life of the company, pictures and everything."

Then he gave me his phone number back east and told me to call if I had any questions. For the first few weeks following his move, we talked at least every other day. After that the calls became shorter and more infrequent. The last time I called another voice answered the phone to tell me that Robert was gone.

Paul and I soon began going to the museum. At first, the ladies — Fran, Jeanne, Betty, and Noreen — were welcoming but a little distant, not knowing whether to trust us. Slowly we gained their confidence and cooperation, and we were allowed to wander at will throughout the museum. At one point, Paul brought in a professional photographer to take color photos of the make-up rooms, various Factor products, and memorabilia from the past. We also met several times with the spokesperson for the family, Barbara Factor Bentley, Davis's daughter, to introduce ourselves, let her know of our involvement through Robert, and progress.

There were many visits to the museum on my own, as well as to the Mormon Temple Family History Library in West Los Angeles, and Max's early home in Boyle Heights, where I was given a grand tour by the current owner.

Max Factor: The Man Who Changed the Faces of the World is the first popular biography of the make-up master and the company he founded. Because it is primarily based on Robert Salvatore's exhaustive research, this book is dedicated to him.

Acknowledgments

*H*ow do you thank scores of people you don't know or have never met? They were the people who wrote so many of the detailed and invaluable documents, memos, reports, and bulletins about what took place long ago at Max Factor and Company, information that was stored away and was unseen by human eyes for decades. Then there were the reporters, named and uncredited, who wrote the hundreds of articles about Max Factor in newspapers and magazines dating back to his early years in Hollywood. I wish to thank Procter & Gamble Company for providing access to the Max Factor archives.

There are also the individuals I met when I first began researching the Max Factor biography, and continued to meet over the years, who have generously provided me with stories, anecdotes, and assistance that wouldn't have been available to me through any other source.

Many, many thanks and appreciation to: Barbara Factor Bentley, Joseph Bentley, Carroll A. Bodie, the Max Factor Family Foundation, Donelle Dadigan, the Boyle Heights Chamber of Commerce, Amy Fischer, Noreen Hinds, Betty Jennings, Paul

A. Kaufman, Randy Koss, Betty Lasky, Audrey P. Meltzer, the Missouri Historical Society, Jay Morganstern, Raúl Polit, Ed Rider, Liz Roberson, Josephine Salvatore, Leo Salvatore, Jane Seymour, Fran Tygel, Jeanne Veloz . . . and Robert Salvatore. Finally, a big nod to my publisher, Richard Seaver, and eagle-eyed editor, Casey Ebro. I couldn't have done it without any of you!